# Collected

Collecting Everyday Moments
and Centering Them on
the Gospel of Jesus Christ

Joy Bice

*Collected*

Copyright © 2014 by Joy Bice

All rights reserved. No part of this publication may be reproduced, stored in retrieval system or transmitted in any form by any means, electronic, mechanical, photocopy, recording or otherwise, without the prior permission of the publisher, except as provided for by USA copyright law.

First Edition, December 2014.

Printed in the United States of America

Scripture quotations are from the ESV® Bible (The Holy Bible, English Standard Version®), copyright ©2001 by Crossway, a publishing ministry of Good News Publishers. Used by permission. All rights reserved.

All emphasis in Scripture quotations has been added by the author.

ISBN: 1502335301

EAN-13: 978-1502335302

Cover Photo: Josiah D. Bice Photography

To the ladies of Sovereign Grace Church,
Bellbrook, OH

With much love and appreciation.

## Table of Contents

Acknowledgements ................................................................................... 7
Introduction ............................................................................................... 9
Look For The Gospel .............................................................................. 11
Eternal Life Is Not A Consolation Prize ................................................ 13
Fridges and Fruit ..................................................................................... 15
Life Is Tiring ............................................................................................ 17
How To Move Your Wagon .................................................................... 19
The Top Of My To-Do List .................................................................... 23
Put Out Your Torch ................................................................................ 25
Making Peace With Imperfection .......................................................... 27
Count It All Joy ....................................................................................... 29
Ups and Downs ....................................................................................... 32
Paralyzed .................................................................................................. 34
One Month's Rent ................................................................................... 36
Things We Leave Behind ........................................................................ 39
Heart, Idols and Hope ............................................................................ 41
Thoughts About Conflict ........................................................................ 45
A Peaceful Soul ....................................................................................... 47
Change is Simple, But Hard! .................................................................. 49
Right Where You Belong ....................................................................... 51
Life In A Garden ..................................................................................... 53
Victory in Disguise .................................................................................. 55
Anchored By The Gospel ....................................................................... 57
Clinging To The Cross ............................................................................ 59
Be Careful to Be Carefree ...................................................................... 62
Am I a Beautiful Mess? ........................................................................... 65
Looking Back, Looking Forward ........................................................... 67
Right Suspicions ...................................................................................... 71

Surprising Similarities Between India and Preschool .......................................... 73

Smile Lines ........................................................................................................... 75

Love The Word ..................................................................................................... 77

Pride ..................................................................................................................... 81

Lessons From A Shrew ......................................................................................... 85

Perspective ........................................................................................................... 87

Whatever My God Ordains is Right ...................................................................... 89

Victory .................................................................................................................. 91

Joyful Killing Fields ............................................................................................. 93

May Your Joy Be Full ........................................................................................... 95

The Struggle Is Real .............................................................................................. 97

What Does It Look Like to Fight? ...................................................................... 101

Fear Not .............................................................................................................. 103

Ask For The Spirit! ............................................................................................. 107

Never Forsaken ................................................................................................... 109

Finding Contentment In God's Will ................................................................... 113

Holy Discontent .................................................................................................. 115

A Spot On The Team .......................................................................................... 119

Free ..................................................................................................................... 121

Trusting the Unshakable Refuge ......................................................................... 125

Always Learning ................................................................................................. 129

Appendix ............................................................................................................ 131

Notes ................................................................................................................... 133

## Acknowledgements

Throughout my life many people have encouraged me to write. They are too numerous to mention by name yet I am grateful. I want to acknowledge that my husband Steve would be at the top of that list. He has faithfully walked with me through each of the things I have written about in this book. He has inspired me to think about my writing as a means to serve our local church. He has been patient with my frequent self-doubt.

My dear friend Karalee took time out of a very busy schedule to work on editing this book. That was not a small task! Her expertise and wise suggestions, I hope, will serve not only this book but also any writing I do in the future.

I have had the privilege to sit under gospel saturated preaching especially over the last several years. This preaching has done much to grow my love for Jesus and fuel the things I have written about. Rick, Mark, CJ, Jeff, and Steve have been the pastors feeding me a steady diet of gospel truth. I am profoundly grateful for their faithfulness to Christ-centered preaching week after week.

I am also grateful to Becca, Grace and Josiah. They love their mama and have been a source of joy to me through the ups and downs that I have written about. They have encouraged my writing and have been a means of grace to me in more ways than I can express.

## Introduction

Changing cities. Changing careers. Changing jobs. Changing jobs again (and changing again two more times). Changing seasons of life as a mom. Changing seasons of life as a friend. This book is a collection of how the Lord has carried me through each and every change, and an encouragement for how he can carry you through the changes you will face, too.

With all of the changes that have taken place in my life throughout the last few years, I've thought quite a bit about what I am called to in this season of my life. What it boils down to is this: besides my relationship with the Savior, I am called to love and encourage my husband and to help him in his role as a pastor. This typically means praying for him regularly as well as praying for the church, being a sounding board for him, speaking truth to him, and making sure that he does not slip into self-sufficiency by encouraging him in the gospel. I am also called to the family God has given me, serving our local church, and seeking to build relationships for the purpose of sharing the good news of Jesus with those I rub shoulders with.

I have been encouraged through the years by watching other pastor's wives, and remembering that there is no "one size fits all" pastor's wife. Each woman has her own personality and gifting. Some may be geared to heading up compassion ministries, others excel at teaching women, and others are focused on a season of training children. Since moving to Ohio, it has been my desire to focus on the women of our church. One way Steve has encouraged me to do this is by writing for our church blog. I have loved to write since childhood, and in the last 8 years, writing to encourage others in the gospel has been a growing passion. This book is an attempt to collect those writings in one place.

The second meaning of the title *Collected* has to do with a state of mind. Every day we face a fight to collect our thoughts and center them on the gospel. Because this collection is taken from several years of my life I may refer to having young children, working outside the home, homeschooling, being a pastor's wife, struggling financially, having grown children, moving, or other things that I have personally walked through. Please don't make the mistake of glossing over the point if you cannot personally relate with my examples. We all need to think more about how Jesus Christ affects our daily lives. Your experiences will be different than mine, but we all have in common the need to look to our Savior daily and find our hope and joy in him!

# 1
# Look For The Gospel

January 31, 2009

When my husband Steve became the associate pastor at our church in Minnesota, he replaced a pastor that God used in our lives more than any other up to that point. Why was his influence on us so profound? Because that pastor, Mark Alderton, continually pointed us to the gospel during a time when our eyes were being opened to the glorious truths found there.

One way Mark's ministry affected me personally was through a seminar he taught on Bible study and interpretation. Toward the end of the seminar, he made a very simple statement that had a huge impact on the way I read my Bible. He said, "When you read the Bible, always look for the gospel." That's it, no magic formula, just an admonition to look for the gospel. He had, of course, prior to that statement spent time teaching us how the Bible is God's story of redemption and that it all points to Christ.

Not long after Mark's seminar, I was reading the book of Hebrews. What had once been a somewhat confusing book to me came alive with the gospel. By the time I finished reading it, I was in complete awe of Jesus. I will never forget that experience. And as I read the rest of the New Testament that year, that enlightening experience continued.

But I have to admit I was skeptical. After all, I was reading the New Testament, full of direct references to Jesus. Would reading the Old Testament be the same experience? YES! I read slowly, only about a chapter a day, so I'm only midway through my second time reading the Old Testament. But I'm still seeing Christ *all over it*. If you could peek at the notes in the margin of my journaling bible you'd see scribbles full of thankfulness for the gospel. Here is one example.

In Jeremiah chapter 14, the Israelites were in a very scary place-- scarier than anything a believer will ever face. They were under the wrath of God. Jeremiah writes in verse 10, "Thus says the lord concerning this people: 'They have loved to wander thus; they have not restrained their feet; therefore the

Lord does not accept them; now he will remember their iniquity and punish their sins" (Jer. 14:10).

He goes on to say how he will punish them in verse 12, "But I will consume them by the sword, by famine, and by pestilence."

I think that God would want to remind us that he is completely righteous and just. His punishment is deserved. It is not harsh or unfair.

I think he would also want to remind us that we deserve this same punishment. The fact that we will not see it is purely by God's grace and mercy and has nothing to do with our goodness – in fact it is despite our sinfulness.

Because of Jesus alone, we find ourselves in a very different place where God says to us that he will accept us as his children; he will remember our iniquities no more because Jesus took the punishment for our sins. What can we do but praise Him? We have been spared the greatest trial anyone could ever face because of the gift of faith in Jesus.

How thankful I am for the depths of truth found in the gospel and how thankful I am for men and women who faithfully proclaim it. May I be counted in their number by God's grace, mining the Bible for all the precious revelations of Christ that are to be found there.

Sometimes we are tempted to see the Bible simply as a book of rules, or as a book full of God's harshness towards those who are disobedient. But the gospel thread in the Bible shows us that the Bible is all about mercy; God's mercy poured out on those who don't deserve it. These topics are hard things to grapple with, but they are never apart from God's loving heart.

How about you? When you read and study your Bible, do you see it as a revelation of Jesus Christ? Are you freshly aware of the awesomeness of God and who you are in light of that? Do these truths fill your heart with praise for God's favor on you through Jesus Christ? If not, pray for this and keep on seeking him in his word.

## 2
## Eternal Life Is Not A Consolation Prize

March 6, 2009

God spoke to me one morning about my attitude. I was reading along in Jeremiah 45, God's message to Baruch, the scribe who was assigned to write down all of the messages from the Lord that were spoken through the prophet Jeremiah. He says to Baruch in verse 5: "And do you seek great things for yourself? Seek them not...." Why was he not supposed to seek them? The verse goes on to say that God is bringing destruction on the land (he has a bigger purpose) and that Baruch will be given his life as a prize of war. Here is where I discovered my attitude – I felt a bit sorry for Baruch. My thinking went like this: "poor Baruch has to content himself with only his life." The sound effects in my head would have sounded like a needle scratching a record as I think, "whoa, wait a minute, something is not right with that attitude."

First, the God of the universe just gave a very personal message to Baruch. That in itself is astounding. Furthermore, he has promised to give him his life as a prize of war in a situation that is very dire – life and death. In a life and death situation I would be very grateful to have my life preserved. I was thinking Baruch got the consolation prize, personal greatness versus salvation.

How often I am guilty of this sinful thinking in my own life. When things are not going smoothly for me, (I'm seeking great things for myself) I will struggle to find joy in the gospel that says God has given me life. I clearly don't understand the dire circumstances I have been saved from. God is causing destruction on all those against him and for some reason he has promised me my life as a prize of war. This is not consolation prize! This is not about my greatness but about *his* greatness. What joy fills my heart when I have a right understanding of this truth.

Rejoicing in the gospel, my salvation, is having an eternal perspective (Col. 3:1–4). It is seeking first the kingdom of heaven and his righteousness to which I cling, (Matt. 6:33); not seeking great things for myself whatever that may entail. It's having the same attitude of Christ Jesus who did not seek personal greatness but humbled himself to become a servant and to be obedient even to death (Phil. 2:7–9). It's thanking God for my salvation, a prize of war, and clinging to future promises.

How often I seek great things for myself. God's message is: "SEEK THEM NOT."

## 3
## Fridges and Fruit

January 3, 2008

Several years ago, Steve signed up for a drawing at the grocery store. He did not even know what the prize was and he barely remembered signing up. So a few weeks later, we were surprised to get a call announcing that we had won a new refrigerator. It was exciting to me. I daydreamed about what the new fridge would be like. I anxiously waited for the day that we made the transfer; and as it turned out, we even rearranged the kitchen a bit in the process.

At last the new fridge was in place, the kitchen was reorganized, and it was time to load it up with food. It would be more accurate to say it was time to transfer the food. As I was taking partial bags of frozen vegetables from one freezer to another it dawned on me that, despite the excitement of a new fridge and the cool features, I was putting the same food into it. We had not been given a whole new fridge stocked with exciting foods perfectly stacked in all matching Tupperware® containers. I threw out the moldy oranges and the rotten food that had been hiding in the back corners. What remained was still less than perfect - like the ketchup bottles that were half full.

You may ask, "Why is she writing about a new refrigerator and rotting food?" I do so because God reminded me one morning that a new fridge is similar to a new year, or a new season. I daydream about what a new year may hold, what new opportunities or challenges lay ahead, and how this year will be better than the last. I reorganize my life, carefully evaluate my time, and ask God to give me goals for growth in godliness. I believe it's a worthwhile endeavor – though I don't need a new year to do it. A new year does bring out that natural inclination to reflect and restructure my life.

When a new year comes and it's time to make the "transfer" I find that the inside contents are the same. The same emotions, weaknesses, and laziness exist that existed 24 hours ago. If you looked inside of me you still would not see a perfectly organized life with the best quality of fruit inside. You would find that most of my contents are tainted with impure motives, unfinished goals, and rotting sins.

What hope do I have, then, for the contents of my new year? My hope is Jesus Christ! God grants me another year as a gift and promises that he will transfer to me that perfect life I've longed for. In fact, he already did it the moment he saved me. He gave me credit for the perfectly lived life of Jesus (2 Cor. 5:21). The blood that Jesus spilled on the cross secured my forgiveness for the contents of all my years. That knowledge fills me with hope! Now he is patiently cleaning out my "insides" to make my own life something that reflects his (Rom. 8:29, Eph. 2:10) and he's doing it one moldy orange at a time.

# 4
# Life Is Tiring

May 1, 2007

This morning I awoke to the sound of my alarm across the room. As I got up to turn it off, everything in me wanted to go back to bed. (That's the reason the alarm clock is across the room, it's much harder to push the snooze button if I cannot reach it.) It was not until after I had taken a shower and consumed two mugs of tea with honey that the overwhelming urge to retreat to my bed subsided. How I dislike being tired.

Let's face it; life is tiring. I've been homeschooling for 10 years, and I'm still waiting to hit my stride. I'm still hoping for the day my kids will "get it," and still wondering why it continues to be such hard work. My oldest will begin high school at home next fall. How can we ever be where we need to be by then? The truth is that we have struggles with each of our three kids, struggles with academics and struggles with sin. We all mess up frequently.

On top of homeschooling, life is full of other duties: the projects that never got finished, the projects that never even got started, the books I should be reading personally, the books I should read to my kids, the areas I need to clean and organize in my home, the blog I should write in, the seeds I should get started, the people I should befriend, the friends I should encourage, the neighbor I should witness to, the people I should pray for, the menus I should plan out, the home industry I should begin, and the list goes on and on.

My "undone" status will never change in this life. I will always be incapable of doing all that I think I should be doing. I know I am not alone in this. Just in the last week I've talked with three friends who are overwhelmed with life's responsibilities.

Jesus invites all who labor and are heavy laden to come to him, and, he speaks to everyone, because not one of us can ever do it all (Matt. 11:28). We cannot even handle our daily tasks without some measure of frustration or idolatry, let alone the task of being right with God. The solution? Take the yoke of Jesus, and learn from him, because his yoke is easy and his burden is light

(Matt. 11:30).

If a brick stacked on top of me represented each thing I needed to do throughout my life, I would have a pile reaching above the clouds. That weight bogs me down. Jesus offers to remove all the bricks if we join ourselves to him. His easy yoke and light burden is simply to cling to him and what he accomplished for us. Not to have a spotless home, not to have perfect children, not to have a completed to-do list. Just to take credit for the perfect life he lived. What an amazing truth! He tells us we will find rest for our souls. That is *permanent* rest. I am free from the endless striving to be good enough; praise God! I can never be good enough anyway, not one thing I ever accomplish can be added to his perfect work. That is the gospel. Jesus Christ died for my sins, my shortcomings, and my imperfectness.

I know what you may be thinking. The to-do list still exists. Life is not just about sitting back and doing nothing. You are right. But when was the last time you really rejoiced and meditated on the thought that you don't have to do anything to earn your salvation? You *cannot* do anything to earn your salvation. God is pleased with you even when your to-do list is a mile long. If you are yoked to Jesus, if your life is joined to his, he is pleased.

Step off the treadmill with me long enough to revel in that fact. Then, and only then, through the power God supplies do the next thing (see Appendix).

## 5
## How To Move Your Wagon

May, 2011

I suspect that many of you consider *Little House on the Prairie* to be part of your childhood, like I do. I devoured all the books as a young girl. In my middle-school years, our family lived near the location where the TV series was being filmed. It was practically our civic duty to faithfully watch the show. I imagine that I'm not the only one who has romanticized those "simple" times of the pioneers.

Despite the charms of the stories, pioneer life was difficult. Imagine, with me, packing up your entire life onto the back of a wagon and heading off into the unknown. All of your worldly possessions, along with your hopes and dreams, fears and worries, are traveling on that wagon bed with you and your family. Inevitably you come to a road that was rough, or uphill, or muddy, and before you know it, your wagon is stuck. You can get out and push, but the more you push, the deeper the wheels embed themselves in the muck and mire. What are you to do? The load is far too heavy for you. Would you not begin to despair?

This is the image the Lord brought to my mind not long ago while I was meditating on Matthew 11:28–30.

> *Come to me, all who labor and are heavy laden, and I will give you rest. Take my yoke upon you, and learn from me, for I am gentle and lowly in heart, and you will find rest for your souls. For my yoke is easy, and my burden is light.*

I am by nature an introspective, sensitive kind of person. There are times in my life when these personality traits are useful, but at other times they can lead me down a road of despair. This is exactly where I was a couple of months ago. I was at the back of the wagon of my life, pushing and pushing, and finding myself sinking deeper and deeper under the weight of life, sin, and my own inability to rescue myself. Life seemed hopeless. What pulled me out? The gospel of Jesus! Applying the gospel to my situation reminded me again to find rest in Christ.

What is on the wagon of your life? Whether heavier or lighter, it does not matter. We all need the gospel to transform our lives more than we need anything else. Whether we are on the verge of death, bankruptcy, pain, depression, or disappointment; or whether we are experiencing success, abundant life, good health, or a joyful outlook; we all need the gospel. Without the gospel, you are just pushing, and the more you push the deeper you sink. At this point what is on the cart becomes irrelevant, and you are just wallowing in the mud behind the wagon trying to push it out.

In front of the wagon, Jesus waits. If we heed his invitation, he will lift our feet out of the miry clay and we can come to him by faith, no matter how stuck we feel. "Come to me, all who labor and are heavy laden, and I will give you rest" (Matt. 11:28). He's already done all the hard work of freeing us from the pit we have dug for ourselves. He invites us to yoke ourselves to him up in front of the wagon. "Take my yoke upon you and learn from me, for my yoke is easy and my burden is light" (Matt. 11:30).

The wagon is not too heavy for him. He could remove the baggage if he desired but he wants us to experience pulling it yoked to him. When we are yoked to him the things on the wagon of our lives are light and easy, we can accept them.

This is the rest we long for but it is not to be found anywhere other than yoking ourselves to Jesus. What is the yoke? His yoke is the gospel. It's faith in Jesus, joining our lives to his. We need this rest and he's provided it. We can do all sorts of mental gymnastics and self-evaluation and have much desire to better ourselves but it's exhausting and it keeps us stuck in the mud. God holds the key to our freedom in believing in Jesus who is Lord of ALL.

He wants us to find rest for our souls. This is not a fleeting nap or a short vacation, it is rest that begins now and will never, ever end. This is permanent rest! And he promises this rest for our soul when we yoke ourselves to him.

I am becoming increasingly convinced that our main (but not only) work as believers in Jesus is striving to rest in Christ's atonement for our sins instead of our works, or even our feelings. This is his yoke!

Here it is briefly: God is holy, set apart, so high above all else on earth and the only one worthy of our worship. Despite his high status he loved us and took notice of us. He saw us in our endless striving and all our sin, weakness, and ungodliness and he determined to rescue us. He did by his life what we fail to do. He lived for his Father's glory. He walked in humility. He lived above the influence of people. He loved others, helped them and had compassion on them but he did not fear them even when they threatened and eventually killed him. He did not try to be anyone other than who he was, the perfect Son of God. He did all of this and then credited it to us.

He died on the cross and bore the Father's wrath, all of it, because he is holy and cannot accept us as we are. All of our self-judgments have an element of truth to them. We are unworthy, and failures, and needy and weighed down by sin but we do not bear the penalty for those things; NONE of them! Every sin we fight is a cancelled sin.

His death brings us life and he invites us to:

*Come to me, all who labor and are heavy laden, and I will give you rest. Take my yoke upon you, and learn from me, for I am gentle and lowly in heart, and you will find rest for your souls. For my yoke is easy, and my burden is light. (Matt. 11:28–30)*

May we find our joy in this truth and a deep, real rest from the things in our life that weigh us down as we yoke ourselves to Jesus.

# 6
# The Top Of My To-Do List

June 8, 2007

I've been making to-do lists most of my life. I had to smile when my oldest daughter made her first to-do list when she was about 6 years old. Evidently it runs in the family. However, since I moved to Minnesota, I've found it more difficult to keep on task. How do you like that excuse? I've been settled for months, and who am I kidding? I never was very good with time management before I moved. That's why I like to-do lists. It makes me feel as if I'm somehow on top of things. (Never mind that half of the things don't get crossed off.) Regardless of how many lines I check off my lists, I often beat myself up over my lack of super woman qualities. What is my motivation for being super, anyway? Do I have a desire to bring glory to God, or to myself? Sadly, it's mostly about me. I don't think my condition is anything unusual, though, because God chose to save us by grace and not by works (Eph. 2:8-9). We are always thankful for that! The reason he gives for this grace tells an important truth. If he does it all, we can't brag about any of it. God knows it's in our sinful nature to bring glory to ourselves instead of him. He could have just decided not to mess with us, because we are so self-seeking, but instead he chose in mercy to devise a plan that would leave our effort out of the picture.

Reading along in Ephesians 2, however, says that I was created in Christ Jesus to *do good works*, which God has prepared beforehand for me to walk in (Eph. 2:10).

Hold it! Works don't matter, right?

The very next line in verse 11, says *therefore*, remember and then remember again. It's as if the *remembering* is part of the good works that God prepared for me to walk in.

So what am I supposed to remember? I was dead in my sin; I was following the world, Satan and myself. I was destined for God's wrath, I was an outsider not a partaker of God's grace, I was apart from Christ, without hope, and without God in this world (Eph. 2:1–3). That is a sobering list! I never set out to have those things on my to-do list, but that is what I have completed. Remembering what I was gives way to remembering what God did. Just one glimpse in Ephesians 2:13 says, "But now in Christ Jesus you who formerly were far off have been *brought near* by the blood of Christ." That penetrates my heart again. I was brought near to God through Christ.

Remembering makes me want to be content because I realize that I don't deserve anything. Remembering makes me want to give glory to God because my works have nothing to do with my salvation. Remembering makes me want to live completely for God. Remembering makes me want to ask earnestly for more of his strength and power and to walk fearlessly through this life. Forget motivational speeches; this is the ultimate motivation!

From now on, I hope to put *remembering* at the top of my to-do list.

## 7
## Put Out Your Torch

November 12, 2008

I love it when the Bible addresses specific things that you are going through. Isaiah 50 was that way for me one morning. There were several parts that encouraged me, but I want to share just one section here. Verses 10–11 say:

> *Who among you fears the LORD and obeys the voice of his servant? Let him who walks in darkness and has no light trust in the name of the LORD and rely on his God. Behold, all you who kindle a fire, who equip yourselves with burning torches! Walk by the light of your fire, and by the torches that you have kindled! This you have from my hand: you shall lie down in torment.*

There are times when I feel like I am walking in darkness. Whether it is the darkness of my own heart, the darkness of not knowing how to handle certain things, or simply the darkness of negative emotions, sometimes life just feels dark. In the midst of that darkness, God calls to me and he tells me to trust him (Prov. 3:5 and so many other verses). He does not tell me how to turn on a light, but just to trust him in the darkness. He warns me against trying to light my own torch. He tells me that I can go my own way with my own torch, but it will torment me. Trusting Christ to take the burden of my sin, trusting God to give me the grace I need for situations, which seem too difficult for me, and trusting the Word that tells me that everything in my life is planned by a Sovereign God, makes my darkness light. Trying to solve my own situations, and focusing on anything other than him, only makes my darkness darker and my life tormented.

God lovingly shows us how we don't measure up, he tells us that we can't do anything in ourselves, and then provides the best solution possible – himself!

# 8
## Making Peace With Imperfection

January 3, 2009

Most of my life, I have been trying to make peace with imperfection. Whether my own imperfection, or the imperfection of those around me, imperfection is unavoidable. We live in a world that has been tainted with imperfection, and we feel the tension of it. Often I try to make peace with imperfection by trying harder to be perfect. I may look at people, situations, or things and hope to find in them the perfection my heart is longing for. I am always disappointed.

Life is like that, and expectations never fully turn out the way I hope. It could be my natural bent toward gloom rather than sunshine, but I suppose God intends life to be disappointing in some ways. We live in an imperfect world, whether we can see it or not. When we see the imperfections, we find a hidden blessing. Our gaze is forced upward to the truly perfect.

As I was reading Jeremiah I was struck afresh by God's words:

> *But my people have changed their glory for that which does not profit. Be appalled, O heavens, at this; be shocked, be utterly desolate, declares the LORD, for my people have committed two evils: they have forsaken me, the fountain of living waters, and hewed out cisterns for themselves, broken cisterns that can hold no water. (Jer. 2:11b–13)*

Trying to make peace with imperfection without looking to Christ on the cross is idolatry. It's making broken cisterns, rather than drinking from the fountain of living water, which will perfectly quench our thirst. God tells us that this is evil.

Growing in godliness is a good goal, but making peace with my imperfection is not—unless I look to Christ, who made the ultimate peace with imperfection through his sinless life, death, and resurrection. I want to look wholeheartedly to God, and upon his answer for my imperfection, rather than to myself. When I keenly feel the disappointment of imperfection, I want to reaffix my gaze on him who is perfection himself.

## 9
## Count It All Joy

May, 2012

A single Bible verse, or even a portion of a verse, can change our whole direction at any given moment because it reveals to us an active living God. Near the beginning of the year, I began reading through the book of James. Early in his letter, I came across these familiar verses:

> *Count it all joy, my brothers, when you meet trials of various kinds, for you know that the testing of your faith produces steadfastness. And let steadfastness have its full effect, that you may be perfect and complete, lacking in nothing. (James 1:2–4)*

In my Christian life, I've read these words many times. In the past, my focus tended to be on the command to count it all joy. This time, the Holy Spirit prompted me focus instead on this question: "Why does my faith need to be tested?" The answer came to me immediately. My faith is often in the wrong things, and trials show me my misplaced faith.

We know that the object of our faith should be Christ, and we want it to be Christ, because faith in Christ is necessary for our salvation. Jesus told us that the gate to destruction is wide, but the gate that leads to life is narrow (Matt. 7:13). Our faith must have a narrow focus, a singular focus, the person and work of Jesus Christ on our behalf. Those of us who have put our faith in Jesus know this and believe it wholeheartedly. Yet we are prone to drifting (Heb. 2:1). God in his kindness desires for us to have a steadfast faith in his righteous Son. It is the only way we can ever be perfect and complete, lacking nothing. We cannot do that in ourselves. Only faith in the perfect life of Jesus credited to us, in his atoning death that paid for all the just wrath that we deserved because of our sin, and in his resurrection which validated all he accomplished, makes us perfect and complete, lacking nothing.

God provides a way to keep us on the narrow path, to keep our faith in Jesus. He sends us trials. There is not a doubt that we will have trials. James uses the word *when*, not *if*. So what will our trials be? They will be varied, but maybe you will relate to some of these examples.

We will face trials with people throughout our lives. Relational conflict shows up when a brother or sister is hard to get along with, when another person doesn't meet your expectations, when unfulfilled desires *for* marriage or family remain unfilled, when people offend you, and when death separates you from loved ones. We cannot avoid trials with people, and yet relational trials show us that we look too much to other people for our joy instead of looking to Jesus. We are tempted to place our hope in people, rather than enjoying them as good gifts from God.

We will also face trials with material things: not enough money to cover the bills, not enough space in a home, not enough reliability in a car, not enough food in the cupboards, not enough value in an investment, or not enough of anything that we think we need. Again, we are tempted to put our trust in things, rather than enjoying them as God's gifts.

We will also face personal trials that reveal our temptation to trust in ourselves. There is nothing like failure, misbehaving children, blunders on the job, loss of a job, criticism from others, and physical sickness to make us realize how fragile we are. We must depend on God even for our very breath, and depend on the work of Jesus for our value and worth as his chosen and beloved ones. No personal failure or physical sickness changes that status.

If God were unloving and uncaring, he would leave us to ourselves, to our misplaced faith, and to our destruction. But God is loving and merciful and yearns for us to cling only to him. So he sends trials. Our trials are from a loving hand, for our good, and that is why we can count them all joy! We don't count them as joy because they make us a better person, though they do cause us to grow in conformity to the image of Christ (Rom. 8:28–29). We don't count them as joy because we enjoy them, though they do help us find fullness of joy (Ps. 16:11). We can count trials as joy only because the Spirit of Christ gives us eyes to see his good purpose in them. That good purpose primarily is so that we may be found:

> *...looking to Jesus, the founder and perfecter of our faith, who for the joy that was set before him endured the cross, despising the shame, and is seated at the right hand of the throne of God. (Heb. 12:2)*

We fix our eyes on Jesus, so that in our trials we will learn to cling to him, fix all our faith in him, and allow him to heal our idolatry.

Are you experiencing a trial even today? Consider it a joyful thing, because your heavenly father loves you too much to let you run away from him forever.

In the next few chapters, I will share with you a few examples of how God has met our family in trials.

## 10
## Ups and Downs

*(The following was written in 2007 when I was actively homeschooling my kids, then 14, 12, and 10. This is a small example of a daily trial like I wrote about in the previous chapter.)*

The last few mornings I've had sweet devotional times. In reading God's word, I have been reminded how precious my salvation is. I have felt a real joy in that, a joy I long for every day.

But for the last three days, there has been a struggle of wills at my house. Right after breakfast, we sing a specific hymn together and talk about what it means. This week we are singing the hymn *Like a River Glorious*. On two of the mornings, one child has been completely uncooperative, because they don't like the style of this song. The clash of wills has led to an extended time of trials with this child. I can't make someone sing.

So after breakfast, I was already praying for a better day. This morning started out well, with an idea to try singing the hymn in a different style and surprising dad with the rendition during family night. Everyone seemed to like the idea. It started out fun, with everyone joining in. But then the clapping got off beat, and the singing was not the way I wanted. Our time of musical worship ended in anger and frustration. No song – at least for now. I confessed to my kids where I was wrong, but I still felt that, as the parent and music teacher, I had a right to say how I wanted it to be done.

Let's unravel this trial a bit. I was frustrated about their seeming lack of obedience, but in reality, they were just trying to have fun with what I was telling them to do. I had in my mind a picture of the other "performing" homeschoolers and thought that, at least for tonight, we would discover how great we were together. I had in my mind the thought of impressing my husband. I had in my mind pride and self. Somehow pulling off this song would validate and make me a successful homeschooling mom.

How did a precious and sweet time with the Lord degenerate so quickly?

It's only by God's grace that I can acknowledge this sin in my heart. In the midst of my little pity party, the Holy Spirit reminded me of the words in the hymn we were singing:

> *Every joy or trial falleth from above,*
> *Traced upon our dial by the Sun of Love,*
> *We may trust him fully all for us to do,*
> *They who trust him wholly find him wholly true.*
> *Stayed upon Jehovah hearts are fully blest,*
> *Finding as he promised perfect peace and rest.*[1]

How quickly my eyes get off my Savior and onto myself. This points to the fact that any amount of good happening in my life is only by God's grace and by his Spirit. Thankfully, I am justified through faith in Christ. Not only are all of my sins washed away, but I am also given credit for Christ's perfect record of obedience. My nature is to turn to self and his nature was to turn to his Father and do all for his glory. Now, God is making me into the person that he has declared me to be through faith in Christ. Every joy, like my time with him in the mornings, or every trial, like music fiascos, is given to me by the hand of a loving God who is trustworthy and true. Even as I type this I feel peace and rest come over me.

I think I need to go and apologize to my precious children!

## 11
## Paralyzed

September 9, 2007

I received a devotional book for Christmas last year called *Pearls of Great Price,* by Joni Erickson Tada. As I have read it during my quiet times this year, I have been amazed at how many times the devotional for the day went so well with the scripture passage I had just been reading. The thing about Joni that I find amazing is that whether you read her books, or listen to her speak, she never makes you feel sorry for her. You usually come away knowing that she possesses something you don't. While she is candid about the pain and difficulty of her paralysis, she speaks of God's work in her life and the work of Christ on the cross. Her focus on the cross draws your focus to the cross, and you see her joy in Christ more than you see the pain and suffering she endures on a daily basis. What a powerful testimony!

Joni is an example to me, because while I cannot even pretend I know the hardship of a paralysis like hers, I experience a bit of paralysis myself - financial paralysis. I have been pondering this lately, especially after the news this week that my husband did not get the job promotion we had been waiting to hear about for the last couple of months. According to what my husband has brought in for income from his jobs this year, we live below the poverty level. I understand that the poverty level in this country does not even compare with the poverty level in a third world country. I've seen that with my own eyes, and the memories are never far from me. Living at a poverty level in this country and culture has a very different and real set of difficulties though. I feel paralyzed by it. It means less time with my husband, because he has to work such long hours, and even then it's not nearly enough. It means not being able to provide for even the basic bills by ourselves. It means other unfulfilled desires too—like music lessons, homeschool books, and summer vacations – even a weekend away. Every trip in the car has me calculating the amount of gas we will use. Everything my children eat from the cupboards has me saying, "When it's gone, it's gone." I've always considered myself to be frugal, but gone are the days when I could pick up a new item for our home, or a new perennial for the garden. Every baby shower or birthday has me wondering how I can buy a gift. Many times I just don't. (Please don't mention Christmas to me right now!) My parents are failing in health, yet I find myself far away and unable to visit them. It feels like I am paralyzed more than the average person. Maybe this is true, maybe it's not, but I face this paralysis almost daily.

The news about my husband's job has me wondering if God means for us to live like this for the rest of our lives. It would make us dependent on him to provide even the basic things through other people, and I don't really like that. Then Joni came to mind. She is dependent on God to provide through other people every day of her life. As a woman physically paralyzed she needs people to help her with the most basic functions, yet she thrives. She has learned how to be content and even boast in her weaknesses that the power of Christ might dwell in her (2 Cor. 12:9).

What I fight is an attitude of entitlement. Somehow I think that because everyone around me can do certain things, then I should too. Secretly, I feel like it would be easier to be "poor" if everyone else was poor, too. What foolishness on my part! Our lives are not intended to be easy. I am not entitled to a vacation. My kids aren't entitled to music lessons. Truly, I have so much more than I deserve because God has pardoned my sins through the precious blood of Jesus. Can I, like Joni, thrive in less than perfect circumstances? Will I allow God to do the desired work in me through this trial? Will I use this time, however brief or long, to fuel my compassion for others who are suffering? Will I daily find that God's grace is sufficient for me and that his power is made perfect in my weakness? Will I gladly boast in my "infirmities" that the power of Christ might dwell in me (2 Cor. 12:9)? I hope the answer will be yes. I praise God that he is moving me in that direction and I think, by God's grace, I'll get there, despite the heel marks in the carpet.

## 12
## One Month's Rent

June 15, 2007

Since so many of my blog posts lately have to do with money, and I do not desire not to have that be the focus of my life, I decided that I did not really want to write any more on this subject. At least that is what I decided, in my pride, because of fear of what people will think if I keep talking about it. Well, this morning I awoke with a sense that if I don't talk about it, I will not be sharing what an amazing God we belong to and the personal way that he works in our life right now. So here it is, a blog entry that has to do with money. I hope you will marvel at God's absolute sovereignty when you are done reading.

A brief background is in order before I begin. We have lived in this new place for 9 months. We moved because we felt a clear call from God. The rent we pay is almost triple what our mortgage was where we lived before. The job my husband took has brought in very little income. In fact, the last few months have brought in a whopping nothing. This month he took an additional job, which barely covers just our rent. Despite these strains, we have always been able to pay our bills on time and have more than we need provided on a consistent basis. In my mind, getting the rent covered every month is a very basic and real need. We need $1,300 each month to cover this expense, and you can assume that we are starting from zero each month because that is the kind of life we are living right now. So, here is my story of one month's rent.

About the second week into a month, I begin to figure out in my head whether we have enough to cover the rent for next month. All money that comes in, from this week on, goes toward that expense until it is covered. It's not really so much of a worry as it is a practicality of life.

On Sunday our church administrator handed us $100 that was anonymously given to him for us. On Monday night some friends of ours, from where we lived before, stopped in to see us briefly. They put a check for $200 in my hand. On Wednesday my husband brought home his first paycheck from his new job. It was $600.

On Thursday we headed to Iowa to attend a CD release party. My children had the privilege of singing on a children's CD recorded by good friends of ours who are in a full time music ministry. They really wanted all the kids who were on the CD to be at the party, and they even gave us money for gas to get there. Some friends of ours, who live in the town we had moved from, had parked their minivan at our house while they were away on a trip because we live so close to the airport. (We often have people do this to save parking fees.) When they left, they gave us permission to use their van as much as we wanted including our trip to Iowa.

On the day of travel, about 20 minutes from our destination, my oldest daughter recognized a vehicle belonging to a friend of ours who had also moved away. We had not seen him in almost a year. We slowed down and pulled in front of him. Because we were driving our friend's van, he saw the local license plates and wondered if he knew who was in front of him. He sped up and saw us. On a lone stretch of highway in Iowa, he and Steve were trying to yell at each other through open windows. We told him where we were headed and he led us to the house we were going to. As he got out of his vehicle to greet us he put an envelope in Steve's hand. The envelope simply said "Lord bless you" and it contained four $100 bills.

Did you do the math? Just in this last week we received $1,300!

The last part of this provision is so amazing to me. How did our friend just happen to have an envelope with $400 in it? How did he decide to give it to us? We had not talked to him for a long time, so he would not have known our need. We had not planned to meet and the chances of that just happening are very nonexistent. If you heard the story of where he was coming from and how he happened to be driving on that road at just that time it would make the story even more incredible, but much too long. Let's suffice it to say that if we had tried to plan meeting up with him it would not have happened. It reminds me of the time Jesus sent Peter out to catch a fish, and then Peter pulled a coin out of the fish's mouth, to have just what they needed to pay a tax that was due (Matt. 17:27). Only a sovereign God who controls every detail of our lives can pull something like this off.

Yes, I am very grateful that we head into next month knowing our rent is covered. I am more grateful, however, for a God that is so personal and intimate that he carefully crafts events like this so that we can see a glimpse of his awesome power. Things like this have happened to us repeatedly. What a good, generous, and awesome God we have! He is worthy of our worship and amazement of all that he is and all that he has done for us.

> *He who did not spare his own Son but gave him up for us all, how will he not also with him graciously give us all things? (Rom. 8:32)*

An Update 7 years later:

Seven years after this, and other miraculous provisions, we found ourselves in a similar predicament. Steve had just graduated from Pastors College and we had no idea where God was leading us. I was working four part time jobs at one point and Steve was attending seminary and working part time. This time we did not get as much miraculous provision. We waited and waited, and prayed and prayed, and though there were some extra provisions here and there, we were continually having to put groceries and other necessities on our credit card. We were not buying extra things, but still we did not have all we needed for just the basic bills. Our experiences in Minnesota had taught us to trust God for all provision, but God was choosing to work in a different way this time. He was choosing to hold back that which he could have easily given. This time the question became, "Will you trust God when you don't see him working, when the deadline comes and goes without the needed provision?" Our faith became desperate. God used those desperate times to direct us where he wanted us to go (Ohio!), to deepen our faith, and to make us more compassionate, understanding, and patient when those around us were facing times of hardship and God's work was hidden from view. God is providing for us now, and he is even helping us to chip away at the debts we incurred. He was not unfaithful. He is always good. We can, and should, expect him to provide and we can trust him even when he does not provide immediately (Phil. 4:19).

Walking through both of these situations was hard. Both seasons produced tears and questions. Both drove us deeper into desperation that yielded joy in the end. You don't have to be on your last dollar to trust God's provision, but you do have to open your eyes to the source of all you have and see that he consistently cares for your daily needs.

## 13
## Things We Leave Behind

July 5th, 2008

As I sit to write this, movers are at the home of my parents in Northern California. They will be taking a few of their possessions and transferring them to the tiny one bedroom apartment of an assisted living facility. I am unable to help, and that is difficult. The last time I was there was more than a year ago. I boxed up many of the things they did not use on a regular basis, and we sold many others to an auctioneer. They were hoping to move to be near me in Iowa in just a few months, but even our best-laid plans can change. God has a way of intervening when we least expect it. In this case, the change came as a move for my family from Iowa to Minnesota, and the failure of my parents' home to sell. Due to the uncertainty of our future, my parents decided to stay in the town where they are so they would not have to move again.

The last time I talked to my mom on the phone she made this statement; "Joy, it's a terrible thing to have someone hold each thing you own and ask you if you want to keep it or get rid of it." I know my mom has her memories tied up in her possessions. That is why she still has the two rocks that my nephew and I painted when we were five. Every item she owns has a memory attached to it.

My dad, on the other hand, is not so attached to his possessions. He has Alzheimer's and is starting to forget. The last time I spoke to him, he asked me where I lived. At least, for now, he still remembers I'm his daughter. I remember a few years ago, when I visited right after he had been diagnosed. We cried together at one point for what we both knew would be coming…the loss of so many memories.

So, in a way, my mom and dad struggle with the same thing – loss. My parents are tough people. They both lost spouses at a young age. My own birth mother was just thirty-three when she died from cancer, leaving my dad with an infant (me), two teenagers, and a preteen. He remarried a year later to the woman who is the only mother I've ever known. Her own story involves losing a spouse to a heart attack, and four months later losing a son in Vietnam whose body was never found.

Considering all of this melancholy, two thoughts have been consistently emerging in my mind the last few weeks. First, I consider the futility of amassing so many possessions. I once heard it said that we spend the first half of our adult life obtaining things and the second half getting rid of them.

Several years ago, I read a life-changing book by Randy Alcorn entitled *The Treasure Principle*. One statement in particular has never left me. Alcorn points out that everything we own will eventually end up in the dump. No matter how important something is to us, generations from now, it will mean very little, if anything at all. I tried to keep this in mind while I was packing to move to Minnesota. I even bought the song by Michael Card where he sings, "it's hard to imagine the freedom we find, from the things we leave behind."[2] This truth is hard to believe when we are parting with something, or when we are not obtaining something we want.

The second thought I have been considering is about our memories. Only God, who is all-knowing, can know if we will live long enough to lose our memories. When I think about my dad, I am comforted by the thought that when he gets to heaven, the Father will look at him and say that he remembers. He remembers every tear ever shed and every moment. But, wonder of wonders, he also will choose to forget something. He will not remember the sins that have been covered by the blood of his precious Son. He removes those sins as far as the east is from the west (Ps. 103:12).

If it's true, and I believe it is, that my Creator will remember everything in my life, and forget my sin simply through my faith in Christ (Heb. 8:12, 10:17), then I should have a whole new perspective on how to live. Will I spend my life on fleeting pleasure and the stuff of this earth, or will I spend my time investing in eternity where moths and rust do not destroy (Matt.6:10)? Will I find freedom in the things I leave behind? May it be so.

## 14
## Heart, Idols and Hope

January 30, 2009

If I should not follow my heart (Num. 15:39; Jer. 3:17, 13:10) what do I do when I feel the desires of my heart entice me and lure me away into sin, as James chapter 1 says?

God makes a point through Jeremiah that our hearts continually lead us into idolatry. My seemingly innocent desires can deceive me and lead me to worship something else. I see it happen in my own life on any given day.

My desire for a peaceful and smooth day is often mocked by life. Inevitably, a conflict overthrows my plans. In those moments, if I follow my heart, I go down the road of self-pity; and if I stay on that road, I might get lost among the roads of doubt, despair, unbelief, and even rebellion. At that point I am bowing down and worshipping myself.

What if I go down a different road? What if, in the middle of a conflict, I stop thinking about how it affects me and instead begin to preach truth to myself? What if I remember that God sovereignly allows each thing to come my way for His good purposes (Rom. 8:28)? What if I bow down and submit myself to him, rather than act as if he is somehow uninvolved or uncaring? What if I see the situation considering God's redemptive purposes? I have a good idea that the outcome in my heart will be different.

Here is the rub – in a moment of difficulty, I cannot do any of that in my own strength. Not following my heart is the most unnatural thing for my flesh to do. My heart is deceitful; therefore I must learn to have a healthy distrust of it. Even my best efforts are tainted with sinful desires. My heart wants a formula to follow that will get me quickly back on track to a smooth and peaceful life. If I just _____ (you name it) then everything will magically turn to joy.

My hope cannot be in victory over struggle. My hope cannot be in my ability to do the right thing. My hope can only be found in Jesus's blood and righteousness.

Thomas Wilcox says this in *Honey Out of the Rock*:

> *Look more at justification than sanctification. In the highest commands consider Christ, not as an exacter to require, but a debtor, committed to work according to His promise. If you have looked at word, duties and qualifications, more than at the merits of Christ, it will cost you dear. No wonder you go about complaining; graces may be evidences, the merits of Christ alone must be the foundation of your hope to stand on. Christ only can be the hope of glory (Col. 1:27).*

> *When we come to God, we must bring nothing but Christ with us. Any ingredients, or any previous qualifications of our own, will poison and corrupt faith. He that builds upon duties, graces, etc., knows not the merits of Christ. This makes believing so hard, so far above nature. If you believe, you must every day renounce, as dung and dross (Phil. 3:7,8), your privileges, your obedience, your baptism, your sanctification, your duties, your graces, your tears, your meltings, your humblings, and nothing but Christ must be held up. Every day your workings and your self-sufficiency must be destroyed. You must take all out of God's hand. Christ is the gift of God (John 4:10). Faith is the gift of God (Eph. 2:8). Pardon is a free gift (Isa. 45:22). Ah, how nature storms, frets, rages at this, that all is of gift and it can purchase nothing with its acting and tears and duties, that all workings are excluded, and of no value in heaven.*[3]

It's only after I've come to God through Jesus that I can find the true strength I need to do what I should be doing rather than what I *feel* like doing.

Just this morning after I wrote this post, I was challenged on this very point. My heart, idolizing perfection, told me again that I was a failure as a parent because my children were struggling with sin. All of my wimpy responses of, "This is too hard," and "I'm too weak," were wrong, and yet right at the same time. Yes, it is too hard for me, and I am too weak in myself, but by God's grace I can trust that God really has made me right by Jesus alone, not by my parenting skills, and that I do have the power through Christ to do what is right. When my daughter told me that I was too proud to listen to her, my initial indignation and hurt had to acknowledge that she was right. I am proud and it is a fight to respond to situations with humility and not defend myself. Admitting my pride is difficult enough on a public blog, but admitting it to my daughter was very tough.

My children and I struggle with essentially the same things, and I hope the conflict this morning brings us closer in our fight against sin. We *are* on the same side and we all have to fight against the temptation to do what feels right at the moment.

Our hearts are deceitful above all things (Jer. 17:9). Thank God for his complete acceptance, and for his word that defines our days!

# 15
# Thoughts About Conflict

July, 2014

Have you ever experienced conflict with someone? If you're breathing, it's likely that you have. Whether it's someone disappointed in you, someone you are disappointed with, someone who continually rubs you the wrong way, or a full-blown argument with someone, we've all faced conflict.

I can recount significant conflicts in my life, and as they say, hindsight is 20/20. But wait; perhaps hindsight is *not* 20/20. I tend to view past or present conflicts in a skewed light. Often, when I remember conflicts I've had, I try to assign blame. Depending on what happened and how much hurt it caused me I can swing the blame pendulum from my entire fault to all another's fault. By nature, I am a peace lover and conflict is very difficult for me. I'm always trying to figure out what went wrong and how I can fix it. I think taking on the fault is humble, and to some extent it is, but perhaps I can find a greater humility.

When I try to assign blame in a conflict, I'm stepping into a realm I have no business being in, God's realm. Humans are very complex, and our motives are often unknown, even to us. Our vision of other people is usually skewed, and the potential for misunderstanding runs high. Throw sin from both sides into the mix and you have an explosion of complex reasons beyond understanding.

My point is not that we should avoid seeking harmony or humbly accepting blame. My point is that we are not God, and we are not fully capable of finding out why conflict happens. Mystery is at work, but it's only a mystery to us. God is not confused by the turn of events. If we believe that he is truly sovereign over absolutely every circumstance, and that he is continually being faithful to advance his Kingdom and conform his people into the likeness of his Son (Romans 8:29), then I think the greater humility is to trust him, and to worship him in the complex mystery of his sovereignty. He is the one who allows conflict to happen and somehow even designs it without sinning, or causing sin. This is a mind-blowing truth about God, one far beyond comprehension, but full of Scriptural examples (see the book of Job for a classic example).

In all our wrestlings with conflict, we must bow our knee to the Creator. We must trust that he does all things well, and that he makes reconciliation according to the mystery of his marvelous will. My hurts and the hurts of others can be laid at his feet.

Jesus was the only one who ever experienced conflict with others and yet was blameless. He was on the ultimate peacemaking mission to turn enemies of God into beloved children of God, and he accomplished this beautifully through the cross. Is there any conflict greater than the conflict that existed between man and God? Of course not! Then how can I doubt his ability to bring peace between man and man? As I wait in hopeful expectation, can I trust that his plan will be worked out perfectly? Regardless of what my eyes see in my lifetime, can I rejoice that there will never be conflict between God and me? Can I find greater joy and satisfaction in peace with God, rather than the peace I crave between people? By God's grace may it be so!

## 16
## A Peaceful Soul

April 1, 2013

> *The Christian soul is peaceful. Peace is the result of doing something: worry about nothing and pray about everything.*
>
> *If we are alone and exposed and vulnerable then we should be anxious, but we are not alone in this world, and we will never be exposed to God's just wrath. Anxiety is not plausible in this Christian worldview.*
>
> *When I am anxious, I am a functional atheist.*
>
> *When I am anxious, my current belief is exposed. It's not simply unbelief, but believing wrong things about God. Things like:*
>
> *God is not faithful – he won't come through.*
>
> *God is not powerful – he means well, but this is beyond him.*
>
> *God is not wise – this circumstance does not make sense – let me tell you what would work better.*
>
> *God is not loving – if he loved me, this would not happen.*
>
> *We are making pronouncements about God when we are anxious.*

These are some of my notes from an excellent sermon preached by Jeff Purswell, entitled *Counsel For The Christian Soul*.[4] I left church that Sunday freshly motivated to cling to my Savior and trust God instead of being anxious.

Unfortunately, anxiety is my fallback position. I naturally drift into anxiety, not faith. God, in his mercy, often supernaturally gives me faith, but left to myself I tend to see all the negatives and obstacles and then lean towards despair. All circumstances must line up before I am "naturally" full of faith, but then that is not really faith at all, is it?

The day after hearing Jeff's sermon, I had an opportunity to practice trusting God. Monday morning, a recipe for anxiety began to be formed when a phone call from our realtor yielded news that the house we desired to sell is not worth as much as we were hoping. Throw in some self-pity, and a dash of unrelated news that caused anxiety about not only *our* situation but about the whole world, and I was crushed under the weight. Tuesday was not much better. Some time spent with the Lord helped me unburden my heart before him, but my soul was not yet peaceful. Wednesday morning, God graciously spoke to me through his word in Genesis 46, and I was convicted of my presumptions about how God works. On Thursday, I was reminded of Psalm 27:13,

> *I believe that I shall look upon the goodness of the Lord*
> *in the land of the living!*

I have seen his goodness in this life already because Jesus lived a perfect life in my stead, died to pay the penalty for all the sins (including my lack of faith) that I will ever commit, and rose again in power, proving that God was satisfied with his sacrifice. This is the ultimate testament to God's goodness, and I live in the good of this news.

Deep down I *think* I desire to do all the right things for the right reasons, for God's glory. Often when I fail to produce a peaceful heart, or fail to pray about everything and worry, instead I end up feeling bad about myself and beat myself up. Why? Well, because ultimately I want to look good. I want to impress others with *my* great faith and trust. I want to be righteous by doing all the right things rather than relying on Jesus' righteousness. And the way I respond to my sin and my lack reveals this.

Yes, I need to pray about everything and believe right things about God. This is absolutely vital to my spiritual growth! But, I must never, ever, not even for a moment, forget that my right standing before God comes from another person's perfect obedience, from another person's life lived in peace and perfect communion with his Father – Jesus.

So I repent of my lack of faith and my wrong thoughts about God. I repent of my presumption in thinking I know what God will or won't do in our situation, and I turn to that blessed cross where Jesus died for this and every other single sin of mine. I trust him to never give up on his work in my life and in the world. It's this struggle *towards* faith that God is using to grow me *in* faith and not in my perfect reactions to all situations. My reactions keep pointing me to the fact that I do indeed need a Savior. And the great news is that I have one, in Christ!

I am never alone, exposed, or vulnerable, so I have no reason to despair. This is right thinking, and the eyes to see even this truth come from God.

## 17
# Change is Simple, But Hard!

May 15, 2009

My friend, Suzanne, uses a good technique to remember sermons or seminars. Focus on one thing. Is there one thing that stands out, one thing to apply, or one thing that will trigger your memory later? Focus on that.

I have not set out very consciously to do this, but there are times that I find it happening naturally. My brain can only absorb so much, unfortunately, so sometimes only one thing stands out and sticks with me. I find myself contemplating that "one thing" again, and it is beneficial to my soul.

Here is an example. Some time ago I attended a seminar entitled *How People Change*.[5] The teaching was good, and full of examples, but one thing stuck with me. The presenter said that, when you get right down to it, there are only two verses from the Bible that are necessary for change:

*...repent and believe in the gospel. (Mark 1:15b)*

*Trust in the lord with all your heart.... (Prov. 3:5a)*

Let me clarify. The teacher was not suggesting the rest of the Bible was useless, but rather that changing our behavior is simpler than we usually make it.

Do you have a sinful habit you want to quit? Repent. Acknowledge it as sin and turn from it. Believe in the gospel, which says that Christ has paid for that sin and has broken the power over it, and trust in him to give you the grace you need to fight it.

Is there bitterness in your heart toward another person? Repent. Despite our feelings, we usually know that unforgiveness is wrong. Confess that sin to God. Believe in the gospel that tells you how much Christ has forgiven you. Even your unforgiveness is enough sin to cause God's wrath to be upon you, but Christ has taken away that condemnation. Amazing! Trust in the Lord to give you a heart of love instead.

Simple, is it not? Sometimes the simplest things are the hardest. Especially when your feelings go against them. Usually these steps need to be repeated over and over. This practice is not a magic formula for success, but it works because it moves our focus from our sin and ourselves to our Savior. Think about it.

*Repent*. That means we have to acknowledge and hate our sin enough to want to be rid of it. In doing so we are required to turn to God.

*Believe in the gospel.* After we have taken our nasty sin to God, he gives us the antidote – Jesus paid for it on the cross completely and if he cancelled our record of sin he surely will be faithful to eradicate it from our lives. Our eyes rest on him.

*Trust in the Lord with all your heart.* Does doubt creep into your heart when it comes to that thing you have been struggling with? Don't you see? That is because your gaze has drifted from the Savior to yourself. That is why we must always trust in the Lord and lean not on our own understanding (Prov. 3:5). He is always faithful to his promises. If we cling to his character, we find the assurance we need.

Have I implemented this practice perfectly in my life since that seminar? I wish! The last time I was wrestling so much with my pride I felt God reminding me through it, "You know what you need to do, Joy. Repent and believe the gospel. Trust me." Did it happen immediately? Again, I wish! God is patient and he keeps speaking to me about that one thing I need to do. I'm sure he will continue to remind me until the day I die.

Repent. Believe the gospel. Trust in the Lord with all your heart!

## 18
## Right Where You Belong

November, 2014

I enjoy watching period dramas, especially ones that are based on classic literature. One of my favorites has been *North and South,* based on Elizabeth Gaskill's novel. Part of what intrigues me about this movie is that Steve's great grandmother lived in northern England, near where the movie is set. It gives me a glimpse into the life of one of our family's ancestors.

In the movie the main character, Margaret, is removed from her idyllic life in southern England and lands in the harsher reality of northern England during the Industrial Revolution. She spends much of her time pining for life as she knew it. The scenes are cleverly shot, making the South sunny, beautiful, and full of life, while the North appears cold, gray, and full of death. Toward the end, Margaret is given the opportunity to return to her beloved home and finds that it is not as she remembered it. Her comment about that experience often comes to my mind. She says, "Try as we might, happy as we were, we can't go back."[6]

This is a true statement. We can't go back. We might be able to return to a place, but we cannot return everything to exactly the way it was. Life moves on, people change, we change. Discontent breeds this sort of longing to go back. It romanticizes the past. It sees a period of life through sunny glimpses and contrasts the present to be gray and dull. Sometimes we remember only the highlights and forget the struggle. This selective memory must be our sinful human nature at work, because the Israelites struggled with this very thing. Discontent with what God was currently doing, they longed to go back to their days of slavery in Egypt.

Do you long for your single days of freedom? Do you romanticize the time when your children were younger? Do you think fondly of a different place that you lived? Do you cling to a particular work God did in you in the past? This reflection is normal. That does not mean God intends us to remain there, especially if it paralyzes us from living in this moment.

As an almost-empty nester, who has said many goodbyes to people and places that I loved in recent years, I can be guilty of focusing on the past. If I look to the past with either too much regret, or too much fondness, I can paralyze my present. Where has God placed me today? What love and good works am I called to today? What is God saying to me today? Whom can I encourage today? Where is my joy grounded today? I want my greatest joy to be Jesus, and that can happen any time, any place. I can find joy in simply knowing that God has sovereignly placed me right where I am.

I love verse 5 of the song, "Jesus I My Cross Have Taken,"

*Soul, then know thy full salvation*
*Rise o'er sin and fear and care*
*Joy to find in every station,*
*Something still to do or bear.*
*Think what Spirit dwells within thee,*
*Think what Father's smiles are thine,*
*Think that Jesus died to win thee,*
*Child of heaven, canst thou repine?*[7]

To grumble about where we are today is to grumble against a holy, sovereign, wise, good, and loving Father. Think on those lyrics and live in the joy of being exactly where God wants you today. You are right where you belong.

## 19
## Life In A Garden

October 2, 2013

> *The kiss of the sun for pardon,*
> *The song of the birds for mirth,*
> *One is nearer God's heart in a garden*
> *Than anywhere else on earth.*[8]

I love this little poem. I first read this stanza over twenty years ago as I walked with a good friend through Busch Gardens in Florida, and for some reason it has always stuck with me. I have loved gardens, even before I ever had one of my own. There are many things I love about gardening but I want to share a few thoughts from a recent time in a particular garden.

In the late summer of 2013, I took on a small gardening job. I worked for a very kind couple whose home is surrounded by beautiful perennial beds. As I gave myself to tending their garden in quiet and solace, my mind was free to think and pray or listen to sermons on my iPod®. Like the poem above, my heart felt closer to God. When I'm working in the garden, my mind seems to naturally drift into spiritual thoughts. I think this is the reason I loved the job so much. Despite the many sore muscles I had for days afterwards, I felt a communion with God that was unique to that place.

My job was to maintain the beds, but the bulk of my job centered on one large patch of Pachysandra at the front of one bed. From the road it looks beautiful, lush, and green. Upon closer inspection, however, another plant is visible. The owners of the home call it a vining weed, but I remember it from my childhood as I worked with my parents in their gardens. They called it Creeping Charlie. I think that nickname is accurate. Creeping Charlie grows quickly, and it can choke out a healthy plant over time. Its tendrils weave an intricate web of vines under the leafy surface, making it tedious to pull out without also pulling out the desired plant. There are days when I spent two hours on one small area and had only a few square feet free of the weed to show for my labors.

As I carefully cut away the Creeping Charlie, I reflected on how much sin is like this weed, especially sins of the mind. Left untended, thoughts of doubt and distrust toward God, or lies about life and people, begin to quickly creep over the recesses of my mind. If I don't pull them out at the start, they become a tangled mess threatening to choke out whatever true and good thoughts I have. Tending to the garden of my soul requires diligence to keep my soul right before God. There is truth in that.

Then a greater truth comes to mind. I remember that God is the gardener (John 15:1). I remember that he is the one who plants the healthy plants – not me (John 15:16). I remember that he promises to carefully tend to my beauty – reflecting the image of his Son (Rom. 8:28–29). I remember that he tells me in his word that at times he has to prune, but it's always so that I may bear fruit (John 15:2). I remember that he is the one who gives the rain and the sun for growth (2 Cor. 9:10). I remember that he is untiring and does not find the job tedious the way I do (Ps. 121:3–4). I remember that he is committed to this task of gardening in my life until the end (Phil. 1:6). No creeping Charlie can ever ultimately destroy the garden that he has planted.

I remember that life began in a garden. There was perfect communion with God. Sin also began in that garden. Communion was broken (Gen.1–3). Later, in a garden, God himself undertook the task of restoring that communion as Jesus humbly submitted to his Father's will to bear the wrath of all people as he prayed in the garden of Gethsemane (Mark 14:32–36). I remember that God has placed in me the desire to rid my life of the destructive weeds, only because he has first destroyed the power of the destructive weeds. Without his finished work, my work is useless (Isa. 64:3). In the garden, I remember that God is the master gardener. Wise, and absolutely righteous, he can be trusted to patiently tend to the garden of my soul (Isa. 58:11). What joy that brings to me!

## 20
## Victory in Disguise

March 28, 2008

It's been one of those weeks. Ever had one? Nothing in particular is wrong, but everything feels out of sorts. I feel apathetic and overwhelmed at the same time. I know the right answers, but my heart feels weary in the daily fight against sin. I feel the sting of failure over so many things: homeschooling, homemaking, and parenting. I just want to crawl under the covers and come out next week.

I've spent extra time in prayer this week, but to be honest it hasn't *seemed* to help. I have not felt God's presence in the moment of need. I have had times when I could sense his presence through his word. Psalm 46 reminded me that God is my refuge and strength, a very present help in trouble. Did he see my email to my husband the day before bemoaning how I felt that I did not get much help from God in the moment of need? Was he revealing to me the unbelief in my heart and the need to trust his truth over my feelings? Of course!

So this morning as I began writing in my prayer journal, God completely redirected my thoughts, as he will often do. What began as a me-listing-my-complaints session became a God-revealing-his-truth session.

If you want to listen in, here is how it went.

> *Lord, as you know, it has not been a very victorious week. Or has it? Your word reminds me that you are my source of help, and that you are all powerful. Your word reminds me of my great sinfulness and my need for a Savior to forgive those sins. Your word reminds me of my great powerlessness, and my need for your power to work through my weakness. Your word reminds me that all people – even those I love – are in this fight with sin, and that my hope does not lie in them doing everything right. My hope lies in you – who makes all things right by the blood of your Son. I want to have victory in everything going well, not in the crushing of my pride and unbelief. You were pleased to crush your Son, and that is the greatest victory ever won.*
>
> *Help me to see my life through your eyes, and to embrace your methods for my sanctification. Let my eyes be on the victorious Savior who lived through affliction and now stands ready to be my greatest help.*

I hope someday, I will finally understand that God works in the rough times. Then perhaps I will learn to rejoice in all things. This week, I guess I will have to be happy with rejoicing in hindsight. There is always next week....

## 21
## Anchored By The Gospel

July 20, 2009

Missions, evangelism, personal holiness, love, prayer, devotions, Bible study, the Holy Spirit, worship, the persecuted church, self sacrifice, spiritual disciplines, humility, spiritual warfare, eternal perspective, creation, sacrificial giving, hospitality, purity, compassion, serving, joy, faith, and fellowship. In no particular order, this is a small list of issues or actions that have driven me at some point or another throughout my Christian life. I can recall memories of times when each item burned in my heart, some of them for a short season, some of them on and off frequently.

When I look at this list, I see that each item is biblical, and none of them are sinful. (That would be another list!) They are good things. So why do I bring this up? This morning I find myself very grateful that God has revealed to me what was missing from all the above for so many years of my life – the gospel! I was living a life tossed to and fro from one conviction to another without the anchor of the gospel. Those items on the list tended to be full of self effort, desire to win God's approval, desire to be good in and of myself, desire to look good to others, and desire to find a key – a secret to a happy and successful Christian life. Was I a believer? Yes, I had trusted in Christ's work on the cross for me. The problem was that I lacked understanding of the gospel's first importance, of the gospel's power to fuel my actions, and of the true treasure found in Christ alone apart from any of my good works. I cannot overstate this point enough.

Here it the point, in plain and simple language. Through Jesus, I have perfect standing before the Father, because he perfectly obeyed God in every area and then gave me credit for his obedience through faith in him. Through Jesus, I can live a victorious life, because he has broken the power of sin in me. Through Jesus, I can abound in good works, because he has given me power through the Holy Spirit. Through Jesus, I have inexhaustible treasures for this life and the life to come. In the gospel, I find enough simple and profound truth to meditate upon for the rest of my days.

I see more clearly now that my sins can be traced back to not living and trusting in the gospel on a moment-by-moment basis. This is now my life long task – to grow in my understanding and application of the truths of the gospel.

All the years of being tossed about, seeking self-righteousness, or serving with self-effort, have been forgiven. All the ways I have been ruled by sin have been forgiven. All the ways that I have not relished Christ above all have been forgiven. Every moment wasted, and every squandered opportunity has been forgiven. Every day of missed devotions, prayerlessness, unkind words, and self-centered thoughts has been forgiven.

Oh, the joy of having my soul anchored by the gospel! The more I am aware of the gospel, the more I want to tether my life to it. How thankful I am for God's extreme mercy, grace, patience, and leading. Without him my life is nothing, and I have him because of Christ. The gospel is amazing!

## 22
## Clinging To The Cross

November 13, 2007

It all began on a plane ride to California to visit my parents. The man God providentially sat me next to was engrossed in his book. I glanced over to see what he was reading, and was surprised to see that it was *God Is Not Great*. I had seen the book at a bookstore just a few weeks prior, so I recognized that it was an atheistic book. The man was not just casually reading, either; he had a highlighter in hand and was highlighting every other paragraph. Surely, I thought, God must want me to talk to this man about the gospel. I got out the book I had brought along to read. Ironically, the book was titled *When I Don't Desire God*, written by John Piper. In my book, Piper was explaining how any desire we have for God is a gift from Him. I was filled with fresh awe that God had chosen me. What a vivid example, two people, sitting side by side on a plane, in completely opposite worlds. I did nothing to deserve eyes that were opened to the truth of the gospel. What overwhelming gratefulness came over me! I kept glancing at the man, trying to catch his eye, but he never even looked my direction. After reading for a while, he closed his eyes and slept for the rest of the trip. Though I didn't have the opportunity to speak to him, I did speak to the Father about him. I prayed for God to open his eyes to the truth. I prayed for him to see the error in what he was reading. I prayed for God to invade his mind while he slept.

The next week was very different from my usual routine. I spent my days among elderly people. I ate with them, exercised with them, went to Bible study with them, and sat around with them. Two of these people were my own parents, but there were plenty of others as well. I had an up-close and personal look at how many people live out the last years of their lives. What I saw grieved me. God seemed somehow absent in the majority of their lives. Even my own parents seemed to have forgotten the gospel. At Bible study with my dad, the teacher asked a question. A woman behind me did not just give the appropriate answer, which was Jesus, but she said "precious Jesus." Yes! That is what I want for my life, whether young or old – to count Jesus as precious. I was filled with so much resolve to live my life clinging to Christ now while I am able. When my body or mind fails, I want him to be so much a part of me that somehow he will still be on my heart and mind.

I arrived home on a Saturday night and the next morning our pastor preached a sermon about worship, using Paul's proclamation from Philippians 1:21, "For to me to live is Christ, and to die is gain." He spoke of taking hold of Christ now, in this life, with all that we have, so that we can truly say, "to live is Christ." Oh how that truth resonated with my heart!

Then Monday came around, followed by two weeks of what seemed like a fairly regular struggle with parenting and homeschooling. What does clinging to Christ look like when you feel like you are in the trenches of life, dealing with sin? Where is Christ when nothing you plan goes as you hoped? What does the gospel even have to do with homeschooling or parenting, anyway?

Plenty! A song that my husband and I have been playing very frequently these days is entitled *Clinging to the Cross*, written by Tim Hughes. One day I literally sat with my head up close to the speaker, while this song played loudly, praying for God to work this truth in me. What is there in life, anyway, that the gospel does not address? When I have a struggle with sin, I know that Jesus paid for it. When my children struggle with sin, I can remind them of the gospel (and remind myself of God's mercy toward me). When I feel overwhelmed with the responsibility of training hearts that are not always willing to receive that training, I remember that Christ is all I need, and he will never let me go. He is leading me to that place where my tears will all be wiped away. Here are the lyrics:

> *My soul is weak – My heart is numb*
> *I cannot see – But still my hope is found in You*
> *I'll hold on tightly – You will never let me go*
> *For Jesus, You will never fail – Jesus, You will never fail*
>
> *(chorus)*
> *Simply to the cross I cling*
> *Letting go of all earthly things*
> *Clinging to the cross – Mercy's found a way for me*
> *Hope is here as I am free – Jesus, You are all I need*
> *Clinging to the cross*
>
> *Even darkness is as light to You, my Lord*
> *So light the way and lead me home*

*To that place where every tear is wiped away*
*For Jesus, You will never fail – Jesus, You will never fail*

*(Bridge)*
*What a Savior, what a story*
*You were crucified but now You are alive*
*So amazing, such a mystery*
*You were crucified but now You are alive*[9]

In quiet moments of reflection, joyous worship in song, or listening to a pastor or teacher, I see the gospel clearly. What I need most is to see the gospel in the midst of trial. Not just after, but during. Oh, how I want to cling to the cross with my whole heart – and that, I know, is a gift from God. He opened my eyes, and I am amazed at his grace towards me.

## 23
## Be Careful to Be Carefree

September, 2014

I've been pondering contentment quite a bit lately, and the question that keeps coming to my mind is this: are being *content* and being *carefree* synonymous with one another? As I have been pondering what it means to be content, I have been considering that Paul says we can be content in any and every situation (Phil. 4:11–12). Obviously this would mean that we *could be* content, even in the midst of our cares, not just when we *feel* carefree. I Peter 5:7 came to mind:

...*casting all your anxieties on him, because he cares for you.*

Jesus tells us not to worry about anything, even basic things in life, like food and clothing (Matt. 6). This suggests that we should live a *carefree* life. In my pondering, I've been concluding that being content is the same as being carefree, but not in a "que será será" kind of way. Being *carefree* first requires us to be *careful*.

A story from Isaiah 7 will help clarify what I'm trying to say. Ahaz, king of Judah, received some troubling news. Israel joined forces with Syria to conquer Judah, and Ahaz and the people of Judah were terrified. Isaiah 7:2 says, "the heart of Ahaz and the heart of his people shook as the trees of the forest shake before the wind." Their fear was as natural and uncontrollable as the leaves on a tree being blown by the wind. God was merciful, not because Judah or Ahaz deserved anything, but because they belonged to the House of David and God had promised to establish that house forever. In the midst of this terror, God told Ahaz, "Be careful, be quiet, do not fear, and do not let your heart be faint because of these two..." (Isa. 7:4). God began his message with a caution to be careful, not because of the impending doom, but to be careful of the fear or faithlessness in Ahaz's heart. After letting Ahaz in on his own sovereign plan concerning the nations, God said this: "If you are not firm in faith, you will not be firm at all" (Isa. 7:9b). God told Ahaz to be *careful* to have faith. God even gave the reluctant Ahaz a sign, "Behold, the virgin shall conceive and bear a son, and shall call his name Immanuel" (Isa. 7:14). This, of course, is a prophecy concerning the coming Messiah. Immanuel means literally, "God with us." What a beautiful message!

If I could paraphrase this passage, I would say something like this: "Be careful to have faith in Almighty God who is powerful enough to overthrow the plots of enemies. Put your faith in him because he has given us the ultimate sign; he came to dwell among us in the person of Jesus Christ." Matthew Henry, in his commentary on this passage says, "The strongest consolations, in time of trouble, are those which are borrowed from Christ, our relation to him, our interest in him, and our expectations of him and from him."[10]

I began earlier with a comparison of being content and being carefree. Now I'm writing about fear. What does fear have to do with contentment? Being fearful lies behind most of my discontent. I fear something I want won't happen; I'm not content with the status quo. Ahaz feared his kingdom would be destroyed; he was not carefree or content with these circumstances. I don't face issues of that magnitude. My discontent can be petty. Here is a real-life, pathetic look at just how petty my discontentment can be.

Recently, Steve, Josiah and I enjoyed a beautiful afternoon hiking in Hocking Hills, OH. We were impressed by God's handiwork. The stillness and beauty we saw there seemed almost unreal. We had a great day. Steve took a few photos and posted them on Facebook. I've been trying to cut way back on my Facebook viewing so I deleted the app from my phone and iPad. Now I only go on Facebook a couple times a week on my desktop computer. However, the next morning I thought I'd just check it quickly to see the photos Steve posted. My attention instead was drawn to the fact that, in 15 hours, not one person had liked the photos. My thoughts went to the *obvious* conclusions such as, "No one was happy that we had such a good day," "Everyone is tired of us," "We are boring," and "We are not popular." Suddenly a wonderful afternoon getaway with two guys that I love was tarnished, and I was discontent with my experience. As you can tell by my thoughts, I have an underlying fear of man. I care too much about the opinions of others. I can crave affirmation, and Facebook is just the kind of place that can breed more of this longing in my heart. This is one of many reasons why I've been cutting back. A couple of weeks ago God spoke to me through Isaiah 2:22, "Stop regarding man in whose nostrils is breath, for of what account is he?" He says earlier in Isaiah 2:5, "Come, let us walk in the Light of the Lord." God's direction is a much better alternative to the fear of man.

The way out of discontentment and fear is to make my heart carefree. I must be careful to place my faith in the right thing: God himself. Matthew Henry says:

> *The grace of faith is absolutely necessary to the quieting and composing of the mind in the midst of all the tosses of this present time.*[11]

I've given you a petty example of "the tosses of this present time," but I have faith that God is working to make me more *careful*: more *careful* that I look to him, more *careful* to keep Jesus as my foundation, more *careful* to place my hope and expectation in him, more *careful* to believe what he has shown me in his word, and more *careful* to be *carefree*, because he takes great care for me.

Maybe you are discontent or fearful because of your appearance, your health, your marriage (or lack of marriage), your children (or lack of children), your home, your job, your finances, or your life generally. Let me encourage you to be *careful* to place your hope and expectation on God who came to be with us (John 1:9–12), who drew near (Isa. 51:5), who promises never to leave us or forsake us (Heb. 13:5), who promises to complete the good work he has begun (Phil. 1:6), and who promises that he will work all things together for your good (Rom. 8:28). Has he opened your eyes to this reality and given you saving faith? Then you can be *carefree* as you are *careful* to trust him.

## 24
## Am I a Beautiful Mess?

October, 2014

Columnist for *World Magazine*, Andreé Seu, once wrote an article entitled *17 Minutes*. Even years after reading it, I can still remember her point. The article details the inner workings of a mind during a seventeen-minute commute. Thoughts are laid bare and they reveal pride, jealousy, bitterness, judgmental thoughts, self-righteousness, anger, self-absorption, envy and the like. The last line of the article says, "Imagine believing that we don't need a Savior."[12] How many of us would dare bare our thoughts for others to see? Ms. Seu seemed to understand that the things she put down in black and white were common to man. I cringe when I think of the article, because I recognize so many of the thoughts she exposed as my own. We all understand that there are hours, days, and even seasons when we give into sinful thinking. But, if we are truly honest, we will confess that we often seek our own glory, stepping on others as we lift ourselves up.

I consider myself to be a fairly vulnerable person, yet the thought of exposing all the things going on in my mind at any given moment is frightening. I am *selectively* vulnerable. Recognizing my depravity is only the gate that leads me to something more important. I used to spend most of my energy dwelling by that gate, vacillating between one extreme (self-condemnation, self-loathing, self-pity and self-paralyzation) and the other extreme (self-effort, self-motivation, and self-sufficiency). Neither extreme was helpful; neither brought me joy.

No matter how people may view me, the truth is that I am flawed fundamentally, and selfish to the core. Self-evaluation, self-protection, and self-promotion are my natural fleshly traits. I tend to carefully craft my life so that others will see what I want them to see. When they see something I don't want them to see, I am prone to cover it up or defend it.

God, who is perfect in every way with penetrating, omniscient eyesight looks at me (Psa. 139). He knows far more than I do about myself, he knows the ugliness that exists and he sees...perfection. What? He sees selflessness, love, mercy, compassion, obedience, truth, wisdom, boldness, meekness, humility and every other Christ-like virtue. That does not *seem* right and it would not be right were God just ignoring all that he knows to be true of me, and simply choosing to see me in a different light. He knows the depravity and he loved me enough to punish my sin on the cross as his only Son died for me.

My initial thoughts about myself are true. I *am* depraved and flawed, and I fail to love my Creator, as I ought. These truths about me, and even more that I don't see, are worthy of condemnation and wrath. While it might be popular to flaunt our failures and declare ourselves to be a beautiful mess, without Jesus this is not true. It is Jesus *alone* that makes us beautiful, not our uniqueness and not something lovable inside of us. Jesus alone. The fact that God dealt with my "mess" on the cross and mercifully chooses to see me through Christ (Col. 3:3) is the most liberating and hopeful news I can ever hear! I don't have to stand outside of that gate, wallowing in glimpses of my depravity, but I can turn my back on that depravity and walk through the gate of Jesus (John 10:9) into a life of freedom. In my freedom, I can honestly acknowledge the truth about my sin, and rejoice in all that God has done to free me from it. I can work hard at changing because his Spirit is at work in me to make me into someone who more closely resembles Christ (Rom. 8:28–29). I can rest in this truth, knowing God's love for me is secure no matter how I see myself. I can trust God for all things pertaining to my life (2 Pet. 1:3), because he has taken great care to accomplish the most difficult aspect of it already—removing my sin. Now I am not only *free* to obey, but *empowered* to obey (Col. 1:11–14). What a privilege to obey commands like,

> *Whatever is true, whatever is honorable, whatever is just, whatever is pure, whatever is lovely, whatever is commendable, if there is any excellence, if there is anything worthy of praise, think about these things. (Phil. 4:8)*

May the joy of my freedom make its way into my thoughts increasingly until the day I meet Christ face to face.

## 25
## Looking Back, Looking Forward

June 21, 2009

(On Memorial Day last month, I wrote the following):

I turned 40 several months ago, and it's been interesting to me how much more I have reflected back on my life this year, compared to previous years. Though I don't particularly feel it physically, I am increasingly aware that I am closer to eternity. My life may be approximately half over. What a sobering thought. In some ways it seems to have whizzed by. God knew what he was talking about in his word when he declared that our life is only a breath (Job 7:7).

Recently I joined Facebook, though I am not very into it yet. Because of Facebook, however, I have been reconnecting with team members from a mission trip that I took when I was 16. This too has been a catalyst to think about what my life has held since that time. I remember sitting on a beach in Tahiti during that trip and writing these words:

> *When all is said, when this life is through,*
> *Nothing will matter but what was done for you.*

What followed in that poem were the imagined thoughts of an old woman looking back on her life, regretting that she had not spent it for the Lord.

Years later, I read John Piper's book, *Don't Waste Your Life*. How I resonated with the message of that book. One of the greatest fears I have carried around is the fear of wasting my life. So here I am, half done with this life. Has it been wasted? When I look back, I can see the love of self and laziness that has consumed so many hours of my life as I've pursued entertainment and ease. I can look back and see the sins that have dogged me from that time as a teenager. Pride, desire for recognition, fear, and sinful thoughts and attitudes in my heart still exist. I can look back and see the ministry that I've been a part of in missions, in the church, in my own home and neighborhoods. I can remember many things, and I do; yet what has surprised me most as I've reflected back has been the hope I feel.

In my pride, I tend to think that the only way to *not* waste my life would be to do something "important" or noteworthy, as if the only way my life would not be wasted would be if others would want to read about me when I'm dead. Being 40 has made me realize that there is a good chance I'll never be famous, and I've made peace with that. Some of those childhood dreams have finally died, which is not so bad, since many were full of self-glory anyway.

Instead, by God's grace, this is what I see when I look back: a faithful God who has led me, spoken to me so many times in very personal ways, provided for my needs, given me grace through so many struggles, enabled me to be a faithful wife and mother, given me an increasing desire for himself, and filled my heart with awe and worship for him. Only I know the real thoughts and motives behind any of my ministry, which is why I can say all the more that God is so gracious to me. He truly uses the fools of this world.

I have hope because our faithful God is unchanging and will be with me to the end. I have hope, because by God's grace as I look back, somehow I'm seeing him more than me. I'm seeing that *despite* me, God was at work. I have hope because the gospel has been, in increasing measure, a source of true joy to me and I know that it can only be because of God. I have hope because the wise, sovereign, God of the universe will use even me in my quiet corner of the world for his kingdom purposes.

---

I didn't even get the above posted onto my blog because I was besieged by feelings of failure and discouragement (the opposite of all I had just genuinely written about). It felt as if God was testing me, to see if I really believed what I had just written in a moment of inspiration. Was I willing to really have my gaze focused on him, rather than on my circumstances and myself? I am ashamed to say that the struggle continued for quite some time as feelings of inadequacy plagued me. Is my hope truly in Christ, or is it not? Why do I so quickly fall apart at the first sign of hardship?

It's because I need Christ every moment of my life: in the highs, in the lows, and in every time between. There is absolutely no substitute for trusting in the righteousness of Christ. I am *always* in need of a Savior, and must press on during the peaks and valleys of my experience to know that I am only acceptable to God because of what Christ did for me. He lived a perfect life because I can never come close to perfection, in 40 years or a lifetime, and I get credit for *his* perfect life. Amazing!

On Memorial Day, I was caught up in a moment of looking *back* with an uncharacteristically positive viewpoint, but God wanted to remind me that I can look *forward* on a bad day or a bad week or month and know that I still have that right standing with him because of Christ. All that I wrote before is true, and again I need to repent, believe the gospel, and trust in the Lord. I can look back and give thanks to God for his ever-patient mercy toward this fickle sinner!

## 26
## Right Suspicions

August 17, 2009

For as long as I can remember, I've had a nagging suspicion about God. It's been a dark shadow behind every joy, and if I were truly honest, a motivator for good behavior. The gist of it is this – I believe that God is out to get me, to teach me a lesson, and to dole out some sort of tragedy in my life to prove a point to me.

I have experienced pain in life. I've walked through dark valleys in my own soul. However, my pain never quite measures up to the pain that I suspect will be inflicted on me when I least expect it. I have lived with a nagging fear of what might lie just around the corner.

I'm aware of the right answers about the goodness of God, his faithfulness, and my right standing before God because of Jesus. His character *always* does the right thing, and every trial he hands me is for good. So why do I still suspect him to be harsh, angry, and vindictive?

It's because I am a sinner. At the very center of who I am lies unbelief. I've been confessing this to God for years now; it is a besetting sin for me. I know it is wrong, and I desire to kill it. God is revealing to me just how serious this sin is. At its core, it denies the gospel. It says to me that I must attain a righteous standard to earn favor with God. It turns me into a legalist who is afraid of one misstep that will bring down wrath and condemnation. How very opposed to everything I've been writing about for the last few years that is. It's shocking to me as I look at it closely.

I should have suspicions, but not about God. I should be suspicious of my own heart. Somewhere in the deepest part of me I want to atone for my own sin. God forbid! I could never really want this – or could I? This is what my sinful nature says when it wants to earn favor (translated in my mind-a pain-free existence) with God. It says that maybe if I'm good enough, I can avoid hardship.

Specifically, here is what I should suspect about myself. I desire a pain-free existence more than I value Christ. This is a tendency for me; therefore I *must* repent at every little occurrence of this unbelief. I *must* preach the gospel to myself. I *must* trust in the character of God. I *must* do this, not because God will be more merciful to me if I do, but because I will love him more fully if I take pains to eradicate this erroneous belief. The joy I experience in Christ will not have a dark shadow lurking behind it. Oh, how I yearn for that.

Christ's work on the cross for me is done; I am accepted by God because of it and nothing that happens to me in this life is done to me by God to atone for my sin. Everything is done to conform me to the image of his Son.

I echo the words of Sam Storms, in his book *The Hope of Glory,* when he says:

> *I don't want to "be myself," I want to be like Christ.*[13]
>
> *I don't want to grow into the fullness of who I am but into the fullness of who Christ is.*[14]

I don't want to over-analyze why I have these suspicions or embrace the full knowledge of why I am the way I am. I want to eradicate it from my life and move on to be more like Christ. I cry tears of joy this morning because I know God desires this, too. By his grace and faithfulness to his promises, it will happen.

# 27
# Surprising Similarities Between India and Preschool

April 30, 2013

Twenty-two years ago, I travelled with my husband, Steve, to India for five weeks of the summer. We were both twenty-two at the time, and were responsible for seventeen teenagers. I was in over my head, and I knew it. On top of that, India itself was an overwhelming experience. The sights, the smells, the noise: I hated it all. I hated the helpless feeling I had when beggars surrounded me. I hated the upset stomach that I had the whole time. I hated the utter unfamiliarity with everything. I prayed, "Lord, I need you to change my heart." He did; so much so that when it was time to leave, I did not want to go. I loved the country and the people that had once been a source of discomfort to me. I was more physically weak than I had ever been, but my faith was strengthened beyond what I had ever known up to that point.

Recently, as I swept the floor of the preschool room where I have been working, I realized how similar my work experience has been to the India experience. I have only been working at this preschool for five weeks, and my ten-hour days leave me exhausted. I feel in over my head at times, and helpless when a three year old refuses my commands. I came in unfamiliar with everything and made judgments about the place, much like I did in India. Honestly, I was counting the days until I would be done.

Then God began changing my heart. Rather than grit my teeth and just get through it maybe I should view this experience like India and ask God for love for it. Already I have noticed my perspective changing and my heart expanding for the teachers, the little ones, and the parents who rely on these types of facilities. It is not the place I imagined to be twenty years ago when I was so zealous for ministry. But, it is the place God has put me, with people who need him no less than the poor of India. As an outsider, and a very temporary one at that, I am not sure how I can make a difference. Perhaps I will have an opportunity to share the good news of Jesus with someone. Perhaps I am just there to pray. I am there to pray for the exhausted teachers. I am there to pray for the wiggly and sometimes naughty three-year-olds who miss their mommies and daddies (they frequently tell me so). I am there to pray for the families with so much on their plates, juggling work and family and struggling to be good parents. I can certainly relate to that! The need is the same for them as it is for me: to see Jesus, to know him, to be covered by his blood, and to find rest in him.

Wherever we find ourselves today, the need is the same. May God change our hearts and give us grace to love those around us.

## 28
## Smile Lines

May 1, 2013

When we moved to Louisville so my husband, Steve, could attend Pastors College, I suddenly began feeling old. Most of the fellow wives at the PC were much younger than me, and some were only a few years older than my oldest daughter. Suddenly, every time I looked into a mirror, I noticed my age. The wrinkles around my eyes and the smile lines around my mouth seemed more pronounced than ever, and my vanity did not care for it.

One day, Steve turned to me and said something like, "I love the lines around your eyes. They are part of who you are, and they remind me of all the things we have experienced together. If you did not have them, you would not be you. I think they are beautiful." While this sounds like it would have been a response to me complaining about the lines, it was not. It was completely out of the blue.

About a month later, I realized that I had not given the lines around my eyes a second thought, except to occasionally recall Steve's words. I did not look at them with the same disdain, and I even found myself appreciating them. I asked Steve one day if he had said those things about my lines because he knew I had been struggling. He told me that they were just thoughts he had at that moment and he had not even realized that I had been struggling with them. What a gift to me those words were! How thankful I am to have a husband who is naturally predisposed to overlook the negative in me.

Then I got to thinking. God, unlike my husband, knows every intricate detail of each struggle of my heart and he has prepared words *in advance* to comfort me, instruct me, and to make me believe truth rather than my perceptions. He has anticipated my every need. If I would give as much credence to his words as I do Steve's, many of the struggles I face would change. What a gift we have in the Bible and in the Holy Spirit!

The Bible, written as a revelation of Jesus Christ (John 5:39), and the Holy Spirit, whose job is to testify of Jesus and guide us into all truth (John 15:26), are continual reminders of a precious reality. God's disposition towards me is one of favor, because of the atoning work of Jesus on the cross and God's acceptance of his sacrifice for me through raising him from the dead. Some people like to say it this way: when God looks at me, because Jesus is in me through faith, he smiles because he is pleased with his Son.

God has the ultimate "smile lines," and they are beautiful to behold. They remind me of all that we have experienced together in this life and all that he has accomplished for me throughout eternity. The smile of God towards me, a sinner, is part of who he is, a merciful and kind God, willing to go to great lengths to redeem a people for himself. May this reality add many more smile lines to my own face!

## 29
## Love The Word

January 10, 2010

Growing up in a Christian home, the Bible has always been an important book in my life. I was in sixth grade when I first felt a conviction to read it on a daily basis. I was also in sixth grade when I first felt a struggle in my heart. The struggle to read my Bible became a legalistic issue almost when it became a conviction. Reading and studying God's word became something that I knew I *should* do, and when I didn't, I felt condemned. Yet, in the midst of what would be a 27-year struggle, God used his word in my life in powerful ways. God's word taught me and spoke to me through many times and seasons.

For example, as newlyweds, Steve and I were faced with a very disappointing housing situation in which promises made to us by our Bible School authorities were broken. We struggled to trust that the situation God had us in was right. In our impulsive and sinful response, we even considered quitting. Then God brought to me the verse that says, "some trust in horses and some trust in chariots, but we trust in the name of the Lord our God" (Ps. 20:7). I knew the Holy Spirit was speaking through God's word to ask me who, or what, I was putting my trust in. Was it the housing I desired, or him? He used that simple verse to challenge us to stay and trust him for the results.

Another time, long before I'd had much teaching on the sovereignty of God or sanctification, I read Romans 8:28–29. The Holy Spirit showed me clearly that the "good" he causes in a believer's life is being conformed to the image of Jesus Christ, not obtaining something that looked "good" in my eyes. That dramatically affected my view of God's will for me.

These are just a couple examples to show that, despite my legalistic attitudes about God's word, Scripture powerfully influenced me anyway. I had times of desire to be in the word, but I can't say that I loved it the way I do now. Though I knew it shouldn't be, it remained a duty more than a true ongoing desire.

Throughout all these years I was part of, and led, many different Bible studies. God used these studies in my life, but still deep down they did not really change my love for God's word. Then something dramatic happened to me, which I consider to be one of the greatest changes in my life since conversion.

When I say it was dramatic I don't really mean that in the sense of a dramatic *event* in my life, but rather a dramatic *change* in my heart. A night and day difference that occurred in me that caused me to wholeheartedly say that I loved God's word. This helped me start to see Scripture as a gift to treasure, rather than a duty to perform.

How did this happen? First, we moved to be part of Sovereign Grace Fellowship in Minneapolis, Minnesota. The gospel teaching saturated my soul in ways it never had before. My eyes were opened to what it means to trust in the righteousness of Christ alone. Second, my husband, Steve, gave me a birthday gift: a simple journaling bible with space in the margins to write my thoughts and impressions while reading God's word. Third, I attended a seminar that Pastor Mark Alderton called "Feasting on The Word." He taught a principle that would forever change my time in God's word. He told us to always look for the gospel in every passage of the Bible, because the whole Bible is a revelation of Jesus Christ; a story of redemption. It was a simple, but life-changing truth.

After the seminar, I decided to take a slower-than-usual tour through God's Word, about a chapter a day, journaling as I went. Then I came to one of those tough passages in Hebrews that had previously stumped me and caused me to doubt. This time, when I read it, God revealed Jesus Christ to me as someone to hold fast to. He showed me that everything hung on *believing*, not on *doing*. These are my notes at the end of the book:

> *Hebrews has been an interesting book to glean from. I have no idea what Bible scholars have to say about the theme, but I think the theme is Jesus.*
>
> *Cling to him,*
> *Look to him,*
> *Be inspired by him,*
> *Be equipped by him,*
> *Have faith in him and through him,*
> *Be encouraged by him,*
> *Be comforted by him,*
> *Be understood by him,*

*Be cleansed by him,*
*Hope in him, and*
*Put away sin because of him.*

*This book makes my heart want to chime in and say "love him". Precious Jesus, you are worthy. Thank You!*

I failed to really love God's word before, because I failed to truly see the connection between the *written* word and the *living* Word. Viewing the entire Bible as a revelation of Jesus, always pointing me to the gospel, changes me. This works in both the New Testament and the Old Testament. Morning after morning, God speaks to me of Jesus through his word, even when Jesus is not specifically mentioned. Even when all I read about is law or wrath, his word reminds me of Jesus, who took the wrath that I deserved and fulfilled the law that I could never keep. Increasingly, in the margin of my Bible, I am thanking God for Jesus, and spilling out love for him.

At times I still have dry spells in devotions and days when getting in enough time in the morning is difficult. There are still those days when life sucks me in when I step out of bed and I cannot be with the Lord and in his word in solitude the way I would like. The big difference is that I've tasted and seen that the Lord is good through his word and I long for more. I don't feel condemned when I miss time with him, I feel disappointed, and I praise God for that change.

I am grateful that God patiently, through all those years, worked in me to love his word. I am so excited to keep going in this adventure in his word with him, and know that all of it is his doing. What a priceless treasure we have in the Word of God. A lifetime will not be enough to mine the revelations of the pearl of greatest price – Jesus!

## 30
## Pride

January 16, 2008

I am a prideful person. Pride is my constant companion, one I'd like to "unfriend." To work on killing this sin I must acknowledge it freely. Where do I even begin? There would not be enough space in this book to contain examples of my prideful thoughts, even if I could remember each one and write them all down. Pride is there when I compare myself with someone else and find I come out ahead or behind. Pride is there when I feel good about myself because God has used me or feel lousy about myself because I failed to be used. Pride is there when I post on my blog and get a comment either orally or written, or when I don't get a comment. Pride is there when I have victory over sin, and it's there when I wallow in my sin. Can I ever get away from it? How can I even write this post without sugarcoating it, lest you are tempted to think I am humble for writing about my pride?

Here is something from my prayer journal the other morning:

> *Lord I need to confess something you already know. My pride is prevalent. I like to be well thought of. I like the approval and praise of people, especially when it comes to spiritual things. I like to be an inspiration to others. How can I have any impact on the lives of others and not have pride creep in? I'm aware of the very real danger and the very real pride that rears its head. I'm also aware that all of it comes from you – not the pride, of course – but any spiritual life I have. So how can I battle the pride? How can I cleanse myself without backing down from being your instrument? Does it work to just acknowledge this to myself and others and to give you glory? I sense you saying to write about this on my blog. Please confirm this if it is so. I also sense you telling me to confess this to Mary. Please guide that conversation.*

I did confess my pride, and asked for wisdom from the good friend God brought to mind. Her advice was very helpful to me. She reminded me to always thank God for his work, not just *acknowledge* that he's behind it, but to *thank* him. She cautioned me that sometimes looking for horizontal approval with people can mean looking for vertical approval from God, and this is opposed to the gospel, which says that I am accepted because of Christ's righteousness and not because of anything I do. She also told me that sometimes we can want to be "helpful" to people more than really caring about them and serving them.

How thankful I am for godly friends. The more I think about it, the more I realize she is right on all three counts.

God's kindness overwhelmed me this morning during my devotions as he continued speaking to me about this. First, I was reminded in Psalm 14 that there is none who does good; not even one. Then through *Pearls of Great Price*, by Joni Erickson Tada, I was reminded that God's longings and yearnings are always focused on people; not on things or on self. "Never does he express a longing to benefit himself. His heart's desire is to benefit his people that they may glorify him."[15] Then the prayer I read in *The Valley of Vision* reminded me that God is the source of all good. One part says this: "I come to thee in the all-prevailing name of Jesus, with nothing of my own to plead, no works, no worthiness, no promises."[16]

And another part says this:

*I thank thee for thy riches to me in Jesus,*
*For the unclouded revelation of him in thy word,*
*Where I behold his person, character, grace, glory,*
*Humiliation, sufferings, death, and resurrection;*
*Give me to feel a need of his continual saviourhood,*
*And cry with Job, 'I am vile',*
*With Peter, 'I perish',*
*With the publican, 'Be merciful to me, a sinner'.*[17]

Lest you think all this humbling is depressing, I must tell you that it's not. When I focus on my sin without looking to the cross, pride is present because my gaze is on *me*. When I focus on the good I've done without immediately remembering that any good in me is a result of the Holy Spirit working in me, pride is present.

So, I wanted to just simply say it.

*Thank you, God, for your gracious and loving work in my life. Thank you for your example of humility. Thank you for the work you do in pointing out my pride. Without you showing me, I walk blindly in it. Thank you, God, that all that I am has to do with your work in my life. Thank you for Jesus, who paid the penalty of all my sins, who bore all your wrath towards me, even right now as I write this with pride still in my heart.*

*Thank you, God, for crediting me with the righteousness of Christ. His perfect record is mine. Thank you.*

Again, I am profoundly amazed at the goodness of God toward me. His mercy is greater than all my pride, and I have much pride. I am overwhelmed with the thought of how far his grace extends.

As I finished this post and gave it to my husband to read, I told him that I still did not feel like I conveyed the reality of my pride. He told me to just say this: "However much pride you think I have, it's ten times worse." Is ten a high enough number? Probably not, but hopefully you get the point. Only God knows the full extent of it and he has completely forgiven it. Wow! It's a word I keep saying a lot these days. It's my feeble attempt of expressing my awe for all Christ has done. Wow!

## 31
## Lessons From A Shrew

April 21, 2009

My fifteen-year-old daughter currently has a part in the play *The Taming of The Shrew*. I'll be honest and tell you that I knew very little of Shakespeare's famous story, except for the obvious revealed in the title. I was not exactly sure what to expect as I watched the dress rehearsal last week. I had a good idea that it would be comical, and that a shrew would be tamed by the end. I was correct on both accounts. The play was hilarious; the actors and sound effects guy did an outstanding job of working together to achieve over two hours of slapstick comedy at its best. Yes, a shrew did end up tamed by the end. What I was not expecting, however, was for God to speak to me personally through this play.

Kate, also known as the shrew, has a moving speech at the end regarding a wife's duty to submit to her husband. In true Shakespearian language she refers to him as her "lord and sovereign" and essentially says that, since it is his job to care for her, why should she offer war instead of peace? She then speaks of placing her hand under his foot in submission and lays prostrate before him and does so. His response to this is to rise from his seated position to lift her up to where he stands. He then kisses her and it becomes obvious that both parties are blessed by this change in her.

I don't know Shakespeare's intention in writing this play, or if he was poking fun at marriage or the differing roles of a man and woman. Frankly, I don't really care, because I know God's intention for me in watching this play.

I am, more often than not, a shrew. God undertakes my salvation, sees to it that I am protected and provided for, and yet I live to please myself. I offer war, rather than peace, when I don't submit to God's Word, his ways, and his means. When he asks me to do what I don't understand, do I complain or comply? Do I place my hand under his foot in subjection? When I do, he promises to treat me in the same manner that Petruchio treats Kate. He lifts me up to where he is and showers me with affection. He is glorified and I am truly happy. How do I know this? He promises to in his word.

> *Humble yourselves, therefore, under the mighty hand of God so that at the proper time he may exalt you, casting all your anxieties on him, because he cares for you. (1 Pet. 5:6–7)*
>
> *And after you have suffered a little while, the God of all grace, who has called you to his eternal glory in Christ, will himself restore, confirm, strengthen, and establish you. (1 Pet. 5:10)*

Marriage is a picture of Christ and the church. I must not make war with my earthly husband, or with my heavenly one. There is no mistaking it: as one who belongs to Christ, I will be tamed, little by little, throughout my life. The question is, how difficult will I make the process? Will I fight against it and make it more difficult, or will I gladly bow, submit, and humble myself before my Sovereign Lord?

## 32
## Perspective

October, 2014

The secret to being content lies in our perspective. I remember clearly a young woman named Lakshmi, a believer who served our mission team in the summer of 1991. We were in India to rebuild two churches that had been destroyed by a cyclone the year before. Lakshmi had a sad tale of a young marriage to an abusive man who later divorced her and left her with nothing after she put her faith in Jesus. She lived in poverty, and yet she had a joy about her that I was curious about. She served us daily, and on a day when I was so sick that I thought I might die, she stayed by my bedside, nursing me, kneeling beside my cot, and praying for me. She was not the only Indian believer who was like this. Civil unrest, dirty living conditions, sickness and people so poor that they daily went through our trash surrounded us. Yet the Christians had an obvious joyful contentment.

For quite some time after returning from that trip, I contrasted the wealth we have here in the United States with what I witnessed among the poor of India. We were considered poor by American standards, as missionaries we raised support and we usually came up short. We lived in a very modest, low-income apartment, yet I kept thinking about how large it was compared to the little home the Indian missionaries shared. Comparing what we had with what they had gave me perspective and helped me be content.

There is a huge flaw in this kind of perspective, however. It can't sustain itself forever. Eventually our eyes drift away from those who have less and land squarely on those who have more. This is true of all situations in which we need contentment. There is always someone with a sadder tale of woe than us: a harder upbringing, worse physical health, more challenging physical disabilities, and more uncertainty about the future, more heartbreak and loss. While looking at them can produce a temporary gratefulness in us, it is not *true* contentment. There will always be people who seem free of struggle, who have many nice things, who are living what seems to be the American dream, who have what we want. Even in India, there were these extremes: people who lived in a home full of marble with armed guards to protect them next door to a poor mission compound.

No, comparison is not a good way to get perspective. It is based on how we feel and what we crave at any given moment. It grants only a fleeting sense of contentment. In the end it usually leaves us with even greater discontent as our eyes fall on someone else "better off" than we are.

There is one perspective that God gives us, which leads us on the path to real contentment, regardless of our circumstances. It is, of course, a gospel perspective. The gospel proclaims to us that God is the holy Creator of all and that we are separated from him because we live in rebellion to him. Our natural inclination is to glorify ourselves and to gratify our own desires. Both habits lead us to death and condemnation. But God, who is rich in mercy, has acted on our behalf to make us alive with him and to bear our condemnation himself through Jesus. We deserve wrath and punishment, but what we get instead is grace, love, and mercy (see Eph. 2:1–10).

A big part of our discontent comes from not truly believing that we deserve God's just and holy wrath. If we truly believe that, then our perspective in all situations will remind us that we are being treated better than we deserve. As a fellow struggler on this road to contentment I can only offer one solution. We need to fix our eyes squarely on Christ and see him for the Savior he is. We do this through prayer. We do it through reading God's word and reading good theological books. We do it by listening to gospel-saturated preaching and music. We do it by learning the habit of preaching to ourselves when we are tempted to listen instead to our own thoughts and feelings. Learning about God brings more awe, reverence, and understanding of who we are in light of who he is.

Look not to the right, nor to the left, but look up and see your Savior sitting at the right hand of Holy God, beckoning you to come to him (Col. 3:1). Know that nothing in this life will ever compare to that privilege. It is here where you will find contentment.

## 33
## Whatever My God Ordains is Right

April 23, 2008

Worry has been a companion of mine for as long as I can remember. My parents modeled it, and I just assumed it was a way of life. It was not until I was more than thirty years old that God really began revealing worry as sin in my life. Worry can be as subtle as wondering what someone thinks about me, or how something I've been working on will go. It might look like worry about our kids, or our finances, or the economy, but in every instance, worry is sin.

Why is worry a sin? After all, it seems natural that we would be concerned about the things that matter to us. As you know, the Bible tells us many times not to worry or be anxious. Why? Worry undermines God's glory. It proclaims that God is not big enough to take care of us. It says that he is not Sovereign. It's serious!

What's the antidote to worry? Trust in God and rest in his sovereignty. Just this morning I read this verse:

> *Blessed be the Lord who daily bears us up; God is our salvation. (Ps. 68:19)*

This is one of perhaps thousands of verses or examples in the Bible to help us build trust in God. Reflecting daily on the cross also helps because it reminds us that the worst thing that could ever happen to us, the wrath of God being poured out on us has already been taken care of by Jesus Christ.

> *He who did not spare his own Son but gave him up for us all, how will he not also with him graciously give us all things? (Rom. 8:32)*

Gospel-centered music also helps me preach this truth to myself. In the song *Whatever My God Ordains is Right*, I love the line "And so to him I leave it all."

> *Whatever my God ordains is right*
> *In his love I am abiding*
> *I will be still in all he does*
> *And follow where he is guiding*

*He is my God, though dark my road*
*He holds me that I shall not fall*
*And so to him I leave it all*

*Whatever my God ordains is right*
*He never will deceive me*
*He leads me by the proper path*
*I know he will not leave me*
*I take content, what he has sent*
*His hand can turn my griefs away*
*And patiently I wait his day*

*Whatever my God ordains is right*
*Here shall my stand be taken*
*Though sorrow, or need, or death be mine*
*Yet I am not forsaken*
*My Father's care circles me*
*thereHe holds me that I shall not fall*
*And so to him I leave it all*

*Whatever my God ordains is right*
*Though now this cup in drinking*
*Bitter it seems to my faint heart*
*I take it all unshrinking*
*My God is true, each morn anew*
*Sweet comfort yet shall fill my heart*
*And pain and sorrow shall depart* [18]

## 34
## Victory

September 29, 2007

I've been working on memorizing one of the prayers from the book *The Valley of Vision: A Collection of Puritan Prayers and Devotions*. The reason I want to memorize this particular prayer is because it seems to encapsulate the gospel and benefits of Christ so concisely. The title of the prayer is *Victory*.

Last weekend was a tough one for me in a couple ways. The first was the good news that my husband got a job promotion. Praise God! It means fewer hours at work, less physical labor, and more suitable work. Unfortunately, it also means less pay than our already-trimmed budget needs. I had hoped the financial crunch we have been in would be a temporary state, but the proposal signified that perhaps God means for this trial to last longer. The relief I had hoped for was not there. In addition, I received word that my mom's health is rapidly declining. When I received the call, I was not even sure if she would be living more than a few days.

I wish I could say that I responded to these trials with faith and joy, but I did not. I had been praying for God to help me reveal my sin, and he did. I got a very clear picture of my sinfulness last weekend. Pride, self-pity, anger, bitterness, envy, jealousy, rebellion, idolatry, and unbelief all came bubbling up to the surface. Yuck! Thankfully, I was confronted with the gospel several times throughout the weekend and each time it had a healing or convicting effect on me so that by Sunday night I was repentant.

Monday morning I was in my prayer closet feeling emotionally spent, but wanting to "make my soul happy in the Lord,"[19] as George Mueller puts it, by meditating on the gospel. I flipped open the prayer *Victory* and began to read. I felt God speak to me as I thought about the word *victory*. "How can there be a victory if there has not been a battle?"

One idol I fight a lot is the desire for a carefree life. Yet, it's in the trials or battles that I grow the most. However, I don't often view my trials as the means God uses to expose my sin, so that it can be put to death. I'd prefer a smooth life with a perfect image. Is that what glorifies God or magnifies Christ's work on the cross? Is an honest, living example of how Christ transforms a life a better picture to an unbelieving world? Of course it is. May I quit wanting to shrink back from trial and trust God to complete the good work he has begun in me.

Here is the prayer I mentioned above, entitled *Victory:*

> *O divine Redeemer,*
> *Great was thy goodness*
> *In undertaking my redemption,*
> *In consenting to be made sin for me,*
> *In conquering all my foes;*
> *Great was thy strength*
> *In enduring the extremities of divine wrath,*
> *In taking the load of all my iniquities;*
> *Great was thy love*
> *In manifesting thyself alive,*
> *In showing thy sacred wounds,*
> *That every fear might vanish*
> *And every doubt be removed;*
> *Great was thy mercy*
> *In ascending to heaven*
> *In being crowned and enthroned*
> *There to intercede for me,*
> *There to succor me in temptation,*
> *There to open the eternal book,*
> *There to receive me finally to thyself;*
> *Great was thy wisdom in devising this means of salvation;*
> *Bathe my soul in rich consolations of this resurrection life;*
> *Great was thy grace*
> *In commanding me to come hand in hand with thee to the Father,*
> *To be knit to him eternally,*
> *To discover in him my rest,*
> *To find in him my peace,*
> *To behold his glory,*
> *To honor him who is alone worthy;*
> *In giving me the Spirit as teacher, guide, power,*
> *That I may live repenting of sin*
> *Conquer Satan, find victory in life.*
> *When thou art absent all sorrows are here,*
> *When thou art present all blessings are mine.* [20]

## 35
## Joyful Killing Fields

August 22, 2009

Last Sunday, my husband Steve preached from Colossians 3:1–11. His sermon was powerful to me and was very motivating concerning killing sin. As Paul puts it in Colossians 3:5a, "Put to death therefore what is earthly in you." A day later as I was reflecting more on that whole passage, and the one following it, I was filled with excitement about putting sin to death and clothing myself in Christ likeness instead. I could look at all the sins in my heart and embrace the killing of sin with joy and confidence in God's ability to work. As I was talking to Steve about this, he encouraged me to write a blog post about *joyful killing fields*, a play on words from an old movie title. I filed that away in the back of my mind, but got distracted with the task at hand – our first week of school.

There are two strange phenomena related to the beginning of each school year. First, the excitement I always feel is nothing short of miraculous, considering the discouragement I usually feel at the end of the year (in this case, just six weeks prior). Second, homeschooling can bring out the sin in my heart that often hides during our school break. Things like anger, conflict, complaining, harsh words, and selfishness pop out throughout the day like a field full of prairie dogs.

So I shouldn't have been surprised when it happened. A big conflict arose between one of my children and me. I felt like I was in junior high again because of the way I responded. I did not act like a mature and wise mother. Then, just last night I was too quick to react to my husband twice in a row before hearing him out (which would have cleared up everything by the way). I went to bed last night less than joyful in the face of my sin, yet really endeavoring to remember that my faith is in Christ, not my perfect behavior, to make me righteous.

This morning I got out my journal and was ready to repent in my time with the Lord when a conversation that I had with one of my daughters this week came to mind. She had been struggling with a particular sin and was confessing to me that she was convicted not just about her sin but also about her motives for desiring not to sin. She wondered if she wanted to kill the sin because it was not glorifying to God, or because she wanted control over it personally. This made me also think about my motives. As I repented of my sins of the tongue, I expressed to the Lord that I wanted my motive to be based on a desire to glorify him with my speech and extend grace to others. God reminded me again of the joy involved in killing sin. Oh how it is hard to do! It feels so unnatural to respond in a way that does not feed the flesh. There is joy in the struggle, because I am cooperating with the Holy Spirit in my sanctification. Think about that. I am partnering with a Holy God on the basis that my standing before him is already perfect through Christ. I am becoming in practice what I already am by divine act. That is truly incredible! I can fight with the knowledge that I am assured victory. I often don't want to fight at all, I want to be a passive observer and let God do it all without any effort from me. He has not chosen to work that way. I struggle with all his energy that he powerfully works in me (Col. 1:29).

My heart truly is a *joyful killing field*. May God continue to give me desire to be in the battle. Even when I have a defeat, I am assured the final victory! And those defeats themselves become victories when they move me on to be more like Christ.

## 36
## May Your Joy Be Full

June 24, 2014

My name is Joy. Joy is fine as a name, but there is something about it, which I have found somewhat difficult to live with. Most names are just names, but my name carries with it a certain, presumed persona. My name suggests that I should be joyful. All. The. Time.

I did not notice this persona-pressure much until I got into high school, when I started to get comments like, "Hey, you should be smiling; your name is Joy!" Factor into this situation the reality that my resting face is not a smile. I really wish it were, but it's not.

Perhaps I've thought about joy more than the average person because of my name. I have an innate desire to live up to it somehow. That's not a bad thing, I suppose, as the Bible speaks of joy quite a bit and God commands us to "rejoice always" (I Thess. 5:16, Phil. 4:4). He also tells us that abiding in him is the way to experience full joy (John 15). I have found that to be true in my life. When my focus is on what Christ has done for me, then I am filled with joy. How can I not be? God chose me from before the foundation of the world (Eph. 1:4), plucked me from my darkness and futile existence, and transferred me into his kingdom of light (Col. 1:13). God secured a place for me with him for eternity, and gave me the record of Christ's perfect obedience (2 Cor. 5:21). This inheritance includes his perfect joy! I am continually humbled by this fact. While this produces times of joy in me, I cannot say that I feel this joy continually. I aim to experience it increasingly, but like everyone else, I can limit my joy by looking for it in my circumstances, rather than in Christ.

Towards the end of our time at the Sovereign Grace Pastors College, a prophetic team from Cornerstone Church in Knoxville came to pray over each of the students and their wives. At one point, as the team prayed for us, the following was prayed over me:

*Father, I sense that there is something significant about Joy's name. I sense that you want her to know that her name is 'Joy' to remind her that you take joy in her, you delight in her.*

Wow! I had never met these people before, and they would not have known my life of grasping for joy. All this time I thought my name had to do with *my* joy, but here it was, the whisper to me that all along it was really about *the Father's* joy. There it was, the answer to my dilemma. I will never be able to live up to my name. I will never be perfectly joyful. God takes joy in me, simply for his own good pleasure. That is a huge mystery. It's easy for me to accept that I am a wretch deserving of wrath. To accept that God delights in me is more difficult. It requires faith to take God at his word. It requires humility to accept that he can feel this way about me. It evokes worship to think about how intimately and lovingly he is acquainted with me; and, as you may have guessed, it produces joy in me to think of it even now as I write this post.

Dear sisters in the Lord, your name does not have to be Joy for the Father to delight in you. He does. Why else would he send his only Son to fulfill all the righteous requirements of the law for you (Rom. 8:3–4) and absorb every drop of wrath that should have been yours through his Son's sacrificial death (1 Thess. 1:10; 5:9)? Why else would he be committed to you for all of eternity, and promise to never leave you nor forsake you (Heb. 13:5)? We can experience joy by remembering the joyful love of the Father for us (Zeph. 3:17). Be sure to remember this: His joyful love for us is not dependent on us experiencing joy, but by us remembering the joyful love of the Father for us.

May your joy be full!

## 37
## The Struggle Is Real

June 19, 2014

The struggle is real.... I hear this phrase quite a bit from my daughter who tells me it's a common saying among the "younger" generation. I've heard it used as a comic narrative regarding things that don't really matter such as, "I can't decide what to wear...the struggle is real." I have also heard it describe true struggles like, "I don't know what to do with my life...the struggle is real."

As I sit here writing this, I'm thinking about life's struggles. There are many, are there not? Perhaps you are in the thick of parenting young children. The struggle is real. Maybe you have older kids and the schedules have you in a constant flurry of activity. The struggle is real. Maybe you are tired of being single. The struggle is real. Maybe you are trying to get a grip on your finances. The struggle is real. Possibly you have a relationship in your life that is strained. The struggle is real. Loneliness, loss, discouragement, and weariness...the struggle is real!

My lifelong struggle is desiring to take control of my life to make it look the way I think it should. This goal is very elusive. Currently, it comes from our recent move added to a general busyness: traveling for prior commitments, preparing for our daughter's wedding, selling our house in Minnesota, entertaining out-of-town guests, and planning our twenty fifth wedding anniversary. Each of these things is wonderful, but they can make it more difficult to fully engage in relationships in my new setting, which is something I long to do.

It does occur to me that this "busyness" is nothing new. There will always be a myriad of things vying for my attention. However, I'm called to trust God and walk in faith in the midst of it all. The same is surely true for you as well. The problem is that I forget to trust and walk in faith, so my heart begins to drift. My devotions become dull (or even sporadic). What was once a joy and privilege becomes a duty. Then my joy begins to slip. Does this sound familiar to you?

A few weeks ago I had the opportunity to give a devotional at a bridal shower for my daughter. I talked about how the most important thing we can do for our marriage is to make our hearts joyful in the gospel each day. I know the kind of difference that "learning to apply the gospel to all areas of my life" has made, and I believe that advice with all my heart. So I ask myself, "Why am I so quick to abandon this practice at the first sign of struggle?" Well, because there is a struggle *behind* the struggle. The struggle is to remember the gospel, to let *the gospel* be the basis of our joy, to find our hope in *the gospel*, and to let *the gospel* quell our fears and garner our trust for whatever the Lord brings our way. I would like to suggest that it is that very struggle that is our fiercest; the struggle to really live in the truth about who Jesus is and what he has accomplished for us. Instead, we tend to want answers to our problems that simply change our circumstances, rather than our hearts and minds. We look for any number of temporary joys that this world offers to relieve the struggle, but the world's "joys" only accentuate the struggle. If we're honest, sometimes the gospel can even seem like some sort of intangible, spiritual thing we're supposed to cling to but instead find elusive.

These struggles may be real, but they are certainly not new. They have existed since the fall in the Garden of Eden. In his book *Respectable Sins*, author Jerry Bridges reminds us why we deserve the wrath of God. Romans 1:18 says:

> *For the wrath of God is revealed from heaven against all ungodliness and unrighteousness of men, who by their unrighteousness suppress the truth.*

Mr. Bridges explains that,

> *Ungodliness may be defined as living one's everyday life with little or no thought of God, or of God's will, or of God's glory, or of one's dependence on God.*[21]

That's my struggle! That's *our* struggle, isn't it? We can have the best time in our morning devotions, and then move on to ignore God for most of what's left of the day. Our struggles become bigger.

I believe this is why we are exhorted throughout the New Testament to remember the gospel, remind each other of the gospel, and remember the hopelessness life truly holds without the gospel. Our forgetfulness deserves wrath, but we will never experience wrath because our forgetfulness is also paid for at the cross!

I truly want to grasp the joy of the gospel; a joy that supersedes any circumstance. I have experienced that joy many times, but I don't always, and I won't always. Yet God has kindly placed us in his body for this very purpose, that we might *struggle together* as Paul did:

> *For I want you to know how great a struggle I have for you and for those at Laodicea and for all who have not seen me face to face, that their hearts may be encouraged, being knit together in love, to reach all the riches of full assurance of understanding and the knowledge of God's mystery, which is Christ, in whom are hidden all the treasures of wisdom and knowledge (Col. 2:1–3).*

Yes, the struggle is real. But, we're not alone in it. We have one another and the Holy Spirit. Both who, by God's grace, serve to fulfill the purpose of the struggle—that we be directed away from ourselves and pointed to Christ.

## 38
## What Does It Look Like to Fight?

June 10, 2014

I recently awoke with a cloud hanging over my head. Ever had one of those days? You know, nothing is really different in your life than the day before, but your outlook today is dismal. That's how I felt as I awoke. All the little nagging concerns over a myriad of issues began to grow and threatened to blow my faith to bits.

I prayed. I asked for the Spirit. I read Scripture. The nagging feeling of despair remained. I talked to myself and rehearsed truth about hoping in God, not being anxious, resting in the gospel and God's care for me and control over all things. I struggled towards God and left my concerns with God and trusted my feelings to God. Honestly, not a whole lot of change came over my emotions. I didn't suddenly feel a burst of joy, but I did hear some whispers...

*I am with you always, even unto the end of the age. (Matt. 28:20b)*

*I have redeemed you and called you by name. (Isa. 43:1)*

*I have loved you with an everlasting love. (Jer. 31:3)*

*With me nothing is impossible. (Matt. 19:26, Mark 10:27)*

*Why are you cast down O my soul? Hope in God! (Ps. 42:5)*

*Quiet your heart, Joy, before the sovereign, good, loving God of the universe who is intimately acquainted with you.*

Can I cast my all my cares upon him (1 Pet. 5:7)? Yes, he bids me to! So I did, and even though I didn't feel a lot better, I went on to just "do the next thing." At the end of the day, I realized that in doing the next thing, and leaving my cares with Jesus, my emotions had gradually changed. I went to bed peaceful and content.

Our kind and loving Father cares for us and is always at work, even when we don't see it. He is worth struggling through our emotions to rest in him. Fighting looks like resting, and it looks like pressing on in his direction. While we do, we keep in mind always that we are loved and accepted before the

Father because our Savior Jesus humbled himself even to the point of death on a cross (Phil. 2:8) to buy our freedom (Gal. 5:1). We fight, yes, but only because he fought and won!

## 39
## Fear Not

June 3, 2014

I grew up in a state with fair skies, beautiful mountains, and the Pacific Ocean. Growing up in Southern California brought me enjoyment, but it also acquainted me with fear. I am sure that I would have been a fearful person no matter where I grew up, but the more ugly realities of living in Southern California exponentially increased my natural tendency to fear. The local news was inundated with reports of rapes, kidnappings, murders, and even serial killers. A woman in our church was stabbed and killed as she was taking her morning jog by a man who was casually jogging past her from the opposite direction. A gang on the beach killed a guy from our youth group. My brother's best friend died in a car accident when he was a teenager. One of my dad's friends in Los Angeles went into a depression and lost everything when his wife left him (he lived at the park for quite some time as a homeless man). A young wife died of cancer (as did my mom). These people were professing Christians, and this challenged my young hopes that God protected those who belonged to him. It was quite obvious to me that God "allowed bad things to happen to good people" and so I became even more fearful.

As a young woman, I also feared rejection from people. When I *was* truly rejected by people I feared even more. I feared never finding a husband, and then when I did find one, I feared he would die. I feared not being able to have children, and then when I did have children, I feared all the things that could happen to them. I feared not being able to pay bills, and not having enough to live. You name it, and probably at some time in my life I have feared it (and am tempted to fear still today). Throughout my life, fear has reared its ugly head and motivated my behavior in all kinds of ways.

Fear has many other names: anxiety, worry, "being overwhelmed," stressed. They all have the same root: a woeful lack of trust in God, and a strong desire for self-preservation. Through the years, I have discovered that I am not alone in my tendency to fear. We *all* fear something. Your fears may not be the same as mine, but we all struggle with fear. It is one of those "common to man" struggles (1 Cor. 10:31). Just Google® "fear and anxiety," and you will get over 81 million things to look at!

Several years ago a couple of friends and I read through the book *Running Scared,* by Ed Welch. I was aware that my fears were a problem and had begun to admit that they were sin. *Running Scared* was an immense help to me. Dr. Welch points out that the command most repeated in the Bible is to "fear not." If you read through the entire Bible you will see that command repeated over and over to all kinds of people in all kinds of situations (Ps. 37:1, 7–8; 118:6; Isa. 35:4; 41:10, 13; 43:1). If the command was issued alone like that we would be powerless to obey it. We cannot just "will ourselves" to "fear not." And God does not expect us to. Rather, he graciously provides the reason we need not fear. "Fear not, *for I am with you,*" is God's refrain throughout (Gen. 26:24, Isa. 41:10, Isa. 43:10, Jer. 42:11, Jer. 46:28). He is with us. God, the Almighty Creator of the universe, the One who sustains all things, the one who controls all things is not absent. He is near.

Does that truth bring comfort to you? It is certainly meant to. Unfortunately, for me, knowing God is there with me hasn't necessarily been of help because I have had so many misconceptions about him. Unless I am freed from those misconceptions I continue to sink into whatever the "fear du jour" is. If I view him through a lens of my own human thinking, then his ways and means don't always make sense to me. Sometimes I can be tempted to simply think he is not doing a very good job at being in charge. I must seek to know him more (Phil. 3:7-11). I must study God and get to know him as he has revealed himself in his word.

When my feelings tempt me to doubt, the truth remains that he is sovereign, he is good, he always does what is right, and he loves me with an extraordinary love. This is all revealed to me in the Bible.

As one who has believed and trusted in Jesus Christ, my worst enemies have been vanquished. I need not fear sin and death (Rom. 8:2). I need not fear condemnation before a Holy God (Rom. 8:1). I need not fear rejection from the only One whose opinion counts (Rom. 8:33). Why? Because God took great pains to redeem me (see Isa. 53). He was pleased to crush his only Son for me. He condemned Jesus for my sin. He rejected Jesus as he took my punishment on the cross. Then, he accepted Jesus' substitutionary sacrifice and raised him from the dead for me. For us. Nothing can ever change that (Rom. 8:31–39).

All the things I fear now are only temporal, and I have no guarantees that some of them won't happen. However, I do have this guarantee: God is with me, and he himself has overcome all the things I fear (John 16:33). He walks with me through each trial as one who is already victorious and is leading me through the windy, fiery paths of this life (Ps. 23). He lovingly designs each trial for my good and for his glory. When that last day comes, he will be faithful to present me faultless before his throne, where I will enjoy fellowship with him forever (Jude 24–25)!

I expect that fear will be one of those sins that dog me throughout my life. However, that does not mean that fear has to have the upper hand. By God's grace, I want to fight for faith. I want to fight to trust in the One who has redeemed me and will bring me safely home (Job 19:25–27). I want to fight to believe truth about God and his control over all things (Isa. 46:5–13). If you, too, have an ongoing struggle with fear let me encourage you to not just accept it as "just the way you are," but instead repent. Acknowledge your fear as sin, turn away from your worries, and turn towards God. Believe the gospel, for it tells you that your greatest need has been taken care of; you will be accepted before a holy God and your eternal destination is secure. Trust in the Lord with all your heart, and believe that he always does what is right (Gen. 50:20; Rom. 8:28). Get to know God more through the means of grace he has provided: reading your Bible (Ps. 119), praying about everything (Phil. 4:6), confessing your struggle to other believers (James 5:16), asking for their help, and asking for the Spirit to empower you to think rightly about God with the knowledge that the Spirit himself is interceding on your behalf (Rom 8:26–27).

Let's be women who take seriously God's command to "be anxious for nothing" (Phil. 4:6)!

## 40
## Ask For The Spirit!

May 27, 2014

Last month as I was reading through Luke 11:1–13, my heart was stirred up to pray in a particular way. Over the last year I have been praying the Lord's Prayer more often, as it addresses so many areas of life. It reminds me to pray for God's glory and purposes, for provision of needs, forgiveness of sins, power to forgive others, and protection from temptation. However, my recent reading of this chapter had a different focus. After teaching the disciples the Lord's Prayer, Jesus gives examples of asking for something from a friend and from a father. Mingled in these examples is the exhortation to "ask, and it will be given to you, seek and you will find, knock and the door will be opened to you" (Luke 11:9). As I read those verses, my mind automatically went to the material, physical, and emotional things in life that we need. Jesus concludes this portion with a little twist.

> *If you then, who are evil, know how to give good gifts to your children, how much more will the heavenly Father give the Holy Spirit to those who ask him! (Luke 11:13)*

What need is greater in my life than the presence of God? To have him is to have all. When the Spirit fills me, I change. I bear fruit and have a more godly perspective on life. I have faith in God's work, conviction of sin, and power to repent and believe the gospel.

Jesus' promise to pour out the Holy Spirit on those who ask should affect me greatly. I want to take this to heart, to ask the Father to give me the Holy Spirit as often as it pops into my mind. I pray for him to remind me often, because I am prone to forget. He has been faithful to do just that.

This morning, as my eyes opened, before I even got out of bed, I was met with negative, anxious thoughts. In the midst of those thoughts came a whisper, "Ask for the Spirit." By God's grace, I did ask, and I did receive. It was not something mystical or dramatic, but rather a flood assurance of who is in charge of this world, and I became aware of the grace to trust him in that moment.

Trusting God through the Spirit's work reminds me of Colossians 1:9–11. Being filled with the knowledge of God's will in all spiritual wisdom and understanding is a work of the Spirit in his people, and he empowers us to walk in a manner worthy of the Lord, fully pleasing to him, bearing fruit in every good work, and increasing in the knowledge of God. According to Paul's example, we can pray this for each other.

May we grow in knowing that our greatest need, as children of God, is for the Spirit to work in us to bear fruit and increase in the knowledge of God whether you're a single woman, a wife, a mom of young ones, or an "empty nester." Let's grow in asking for the Spirit's work for each other.

## 41
## Never Forsaken

May 11, 2007

Our gracious God spoke to me this morning. It was not a flash of thunder or a lightning bolt of revelation, just a quiet connecting of dots in my prayer closet. His spirit was testifying with my spirit and I was changed. I was not in there for three hours; it was more like 30 minutes. The speaking had absolutely nothing to do with my faithfulness in prayer and Bible study, though I was doing those things by God's grace. I'm getting ahead of myself, so please oblige me to back up a bit.

Here is the background. This week has been a week of faithlessness on my part. Living with fear of the future, hopelessness, and despair regarding our present circumstances has made me question God rather than my own sinfulness. I have been violating a clear command of Scripture to not be anxious, thinking that I have good reason. Rather than focusing on Christ, my eyes have been on my own wants and desires for a comfortable life.

In the midst of this struggle, there have been encouraging words from friends and increased fellowship with my husband as we walk through this together. These are precious assurances indeed, but the real breakthrough came this morning in my prayer closet.

Here's how it played out. I have Psalm 90:14 written on a piece of mat board that hangs in my prayer closet. It says,

> *Satisfy me in the morning with your steadfast love that I may rejoice and be glad all my days. (Ps. 90:14)*

When I see that verse each morning, I try to remember to ask God to satisfy me with his steadfast love. This morning, the second half of the verse arrested my attention. Why do we want God to satisfy us with his steadfast love? So that we may be glad all of our days. That is a self-serving reason, but it's right there in the Bible. Being satisfied with God brings us joy. John Piper may be on to something.[22]

I am reading through the New Testament one chapter a day this year and taking notes in my journaling Bible. This morning I read Matthew 27, the account of Jesus' crucifixion. I was frustrated by my own lack of feeling as I read these very familiar verses. Not ready to go to prayer just yet I pulled out a devotional book that I use on occasion called *Pearls of Great Price,* by Joni Eareckson Tada. I read these words:

> *Nothing is more suffocating, more soul stifling than the feeling of hopelessness. When you've tried every option, it's despairing to think that you've come to the end of your rope with no aid in sight. Hopelessness breeds when we fail to sense God's hand in the hardship, or the presence of his help. It's demoralizing to feel as though God is off somewhere, distracted by the needs of more obedient saints.*
>
> *Hope is built on fact. And the fact is, God never becomes distracted from your life. He never takes time off from tending to our needs. When troubles come, he doesn't back away to allow Satan a free hand. Today's verse [God is our refuge and strength, an ever present help in trouble Ps. 46:1] assures that not only is the help of God available and accessible at all times but God himself is the always-present help in every trial.*[23]

Behind my anxiety lies a suspicion that God will tire of "bailing us out" of our troubles. This in itself is a failure to recognize God's sovereignty in putting us in every situation. Here is where the dots connected in my mind. After reading the devotional, God brought to mind the verse from Hebrews where God promises to never leave us or forsake us (Heb. 13:5). Then God brought to my mind the crucifixion account I had just read. Jesus cries out, "My God, my God why have you forsaken me" (Matt. 27:46)? It dawned on me that *I* deserve to be forsaken. *My* sins are enough to stir up God's justice *against me* and have him forsake *me*. Instead of forsaking *me* he forsook his own Son. I will never have to endure God forsaking *me* because *Christ* was forsaken for me.

Then came a conviction of sin. Why do I suppose God will get tired of helping me? I believe that it is because I am often sinful in *my own reactions* towards the needs of others. I want everything to get fixed quickly for my own ease and comfort. I can get impatient with a child who keeps making the same error over and over, the friend who keeps struggling with the same despair, or the person who does not seem to be listening to the help I try to offer. It is a dangerous thing for me to project my own sinfulness onto God. We are told over and over that God is slow to anger, gracious, compassionate, longsuffering, and ready to help. What is my response? Turn from this sin of distrust. Turn towards the sovereign lover of my soul and rejoice in all that he is. I am never forsaken. Praise God!

## 42
## Finding Contentment In God's Will

September, 2014

In my kitchen hangs a stained and slightly bent piece of card stock. I picked it up 25 years ago at a missions conference, and it's hung somewhere in my home ever since Steve and I got married. It says: "To be content with God's will and way is rest." That little quote packs a powerful punch! It serves as a constant reminder to me that my circumstances are by God's design and that submitting to that reality is the way to rest.

As I read the Bible, I am fully convinced that God is the author of every event in our lives. His sovereignty is unmistakable in the Word. Knowing that he is sovereign makes me desire to trust him and to worship him.

What about the nitty-gritty, day-to-day stuff that makes me grumble and complain? What about the things that take me by surprise and are out of my "control"? What about the things that other people do, and how they react to me or treat me? What about the simple realities of living in a fallen world? What about the normal passages of time, like saying goodbye to loved ones and seeing bodies and minds begin to decline? What about the hardships of everyday living? Can I truly be content? Absolutely. I don't say this because I've arrived at a state of perfect contentment, but because God's word says that I can. This contentment is not automatic. It takes practice. You are probably aware of this from your own personal circumstances, but we also know this because Paul recorded his journey to contentment for us in the book of Philippians. He tells us that he *learned* to be content in any circumstance. "I can do all things through Christ who strengthens me" (Phil. 4:13). This sounds like he had to work at contentment, doesn't it?

What about your circumstances? Do you have a wayward child, a detached husband, or maybe no husband or children at all? Do you have physical pain, or emotional hurts? Do you have financial burdens, a fussy 2-year-old, a leaky oil pan, a foreclosed house, or cancer? Do you have a strained relationship or a difficult work situation? Maybe you've avoided these circumstances, but still you have discontent in your life. Maybe you do what I do sometimes: I big pity party over hundreds of little festering irritations. Though none of them are very significant, they still spill out. Sometimes knowing what I should do, such as being grateful for the many blessings I have, is not enough to remove the sadness I feel. Sometimes the truth, which has the power to turn on the faucet of joy, only produces a slow leak. What then? What does contentment look like in those times?

The answer, though not very exciting, is that it looks like simple obedience in trusting a good and sovereign God. It looks like going to the source of life over and over, and seeking to know him better through his word. It looks like continuing to live and do the things we are called to do in the midst of our struggle. It looks like being faithful in ordinary ways like going to work, cooking a meal, changing a diaper, disciplining a child (again), or serving another person. It looks like not growing weary of encouraging others, even when you feel discouraged, because you know and trust that God will provide the grace you need.

We do these things in faith that God is trustworthy and true to his promises. Remember, faith is the evidence of things not seen (Heb. 11:1). You have that evidence in your life if you have trusted Christ. You know the many times God has been faithful to you. Faith trusts in our sure and certain hope of eternal life with Christ, even in the midst of the weary moments of this life.

Can you be content that a sovereign God ordains your exact circumstances? I read a book by Corrie Ten Boom several years ago called *Don't Wrestle, Just Nestle*. I've always thought that title was a bit corny, but it's absolutely true! When I am struggling with circumstances, the last thing I need to do is wrestle with them. Instead, I should nestle into Christ, my beloved high priest who sympathizes with my every weakness (Heb. 4:15). I should nestle into my heavenly Father who has adopted me (Eph. 1:5). I should nestle into those nudges of assurance from the Holy Spirit. That is what I need most!

May God grant us all the desire to rest in him and find ourselves content.

## 43
## Holy Discontent

February, 2010

A phrase has been rolling around my brain...*holy discontent.* Should contentment be my aim in all of life, or are there times that contentment is a guise for laziness?

I was looking in the dictionary the other day at the word "content" and I found this succinct definition:

> *Satisfied with what one is or has; not wanting more or anything else.*[24]

I really like that definition, and that is what I mean when I write about contentment. In contrast, I found this description of content in a Thesaurus: *fat, dumb, and happy.* This implies a sort of lazy ignorance as being the source of happiness.

So back to the original definition - *satisfied with what one is or has.* The contented life is learning to be content in all circumstances through Christ who strengthens me. This definition is taken from Philippians 4:11–13, where Paul speaks about how he has learned to be content in every situation. He had some varied ones: beatings, imprisonments, and hunger in contrast with plenty, abundance, and favor with men. Paul truly is an example of a contented life, but is he content with *who* he is? I believe so, considering what he wrote in 1 Corinthians 15:10: "by the grace of God I am what I am." Paul accepts that God's grace alone has made him who he is. Yet he goes on to say,

> ...*and his grace toward me was not in vain. On the contrary, I worked harder than any of them, though it was not I, but the grace of God that is with me. (1 Cor. 15:10)*

Paul worked hard at many things. In particular, he worked hard at being like Christ and preaching the gospel. Throughout Paul's letters in the New Testament, you find much striving, pressing on, pursuing, and running the race. Was Paul fat, dumb and lazy? Certainly not! Yet he was content.

Now let's go back to that phrase, *holy discontent.* Is there a way to be discontent with my current level of holiness that does not turn into works righteousness? Paul seemed to think so. So my definition for holy discontent is this: *content with the righteousness of Christ, not trying to add to it, and discontent with the current level of holiness lived out in my life.*

I've spent most of my past Christian life in what I *considered* to be holy discontent. I've had zeal to be a godly person, and to live a holy life, but on closer evaluation my fervor was a discontent of the self-centered kind. I spent much time doing all the things I considered necessary for a holy life, with both pure and tainted motives, desiring attention from both God and man.

Since God is perfectly pure and holy, how could he ever accept my tainted works? I believed that he would filter out those sinful, prideful motives and keep those good ones. After all that's what grace is, right? Wrong!

From the outside, I looked like someone following hard after God, but inside I was filled with condemnation for all of my failures in such attempts. I willed myself to believe that God accepted me because of Jesus Christ, and that he erased my failures, I held such an incomplete picture of grace. I was far from content with who I was and I thought that was a good thing, something that pushed me toward godliness. I could not have been further from the truth.

The first part of holy discontent has to do with not being content to put any trust in my works or myself. Instead I must wholeheartedly believe the gospel of grace that says that my own righteousness will *never* be accepted by God, but the righteousness of Christ will. Amazingly, God has credited me with that righteousness (2 Cor. 5:21). He not only erased all of my failures, but he gave me credit for all of Christ's successes! He didn't filter through all my attempts and pick out the good; he completely did away with all of it and said, "My Son's perfect record now belongs to you".

I must strive primarily to be content with the righteousness of Christ that has been given to me by God and never try to add to it by working to gain favor with God or get his attention. I am prone to working for my own righteousness, but I must accept (and be grateful) that I can never add to the finished work of Christ. I cannot accept the free gift of grace and then endeavor to earn it. It doesn't work that way. I must remind myself, over and over, that Jesus accomplished for me what I could never in eternity do for myself.

One reason I used to bristle when I heard people tell me what I just told you is because I thought it would make me apathetic towards holiness. I would give a mental assent to my need for Christ's righteousness, only to then turn around and work for my own. After all, Paul, who has always been my hero, did much striving, so shouldn't I? Yes, it's God who makes me right, but I lived as though I needed to make myself worthy of it, even though I would never have spoken it that way. Fundamentally, I knew all the truths of the gospel, but they had not really penetrated my heart.

I've since learned that *my main striving* will always be to grab hold of the truths of the gospel. Striving to be content with God's plan for my redemption, to find my satisfaction and joy *in Jesus Christ* and his righteousness, and the sacrifice of his life, which has washed away my sins and made me right with God. I can never add to that. Never!

My old fears were unfounded. Grasping the truth of the gospel has not made me apathetic toward holiness. Rather, it has fueled my holiness like gas on a flame. The grace of God is at work in me to actively cooperate with the Holy Spirit in receiving and responding to God's grace. I am increasingly becoming in my experience what I am already declared to be by God - righteous and blameless.

I should never be content with lack of amazement or lack of joy in my salvation. Rather let me strive to live out this definition of holy discontent:

> *My amazement and joy over the grace I have received from God through salvation fuels the grace that works in me to be more like Christ.*

Oh what a freeing truth! May our lives always be growing in holy discontent.

## 44
## A Spot On The Team

November 11, 2014

I've never been very athletic. I can swing a racket and return a ball, but that's about the extent of my ability (if you can even call it that). Going to a high school of two thousand I instinctively knew that I would never make a spot on any team. When most people laugh at your athletic endeavors, it doesn't build up much confidence. Add to that all the excruciating elementary experiences of being chosen last for the team, in *every* sport, during PE. It's not even that I was "girly," I was just more of a hiking, tree-climbing, mud-playing, frog-catching kind of girl.

We live in a world where sports are highly valued. If you are good at a particular sport, or play on a team, that almost automatically garners some level of immediate respect from people. I never had that respect, which bothers me and reveals a piece of my struggle to measure up with others.

I remember very clearly the Lord speaking to me about this struggle for the respect of others. I was in my thirties, and actively involved in helping Steve with our church youth group in Iowa. I led a weekly morning Bible study for high school girls. We had been memorizing Scripture and this verse came up:

*Even as he chose us in him before the foundation of the world, that we should be holy and blameless before him. (Eph. 1:4)*

Shortly after that, I was at a winter youth retreat as a leader and plagued with so much insecurity. Most of the other women youth leaders there were younger and more energetic; they had more "in style" clothing and seemed to be generally "cooler." The students flocked around them. How could I compare with them? I just did not fit that cool youth leader image. This may seem like a little struggle, but it was not. It was an ongoing battle in my heart that I had carried around for years. I never felt like I measured up to others and that always left me with either a sense of insecurity or a competitive spirit. Both were rooted in pride.

I was having my devotions on this retreat when suddenly the Lord spoke clearly to me. It was as if images from my childhood flashed in front of me. Particularly the image of always being chosen last for sports teams. In that moment, God revealed to me that I was acting like that kid with my hand up in the air yelling, "Pick me, pick me!" I was doing that with others, but I was also doing that with God. In a sea of people, I had been trying to get God's attention and vie for his affection most of my life. That morning he clearly said to me, "I already picked you. I chose you from before the foundation of the world." I have a spot on God's team and I will never lose that spot, no matter how pathetically I may screw up.

I need to remember this foundational truth that God chose me. Even as I write this, I am again affected by it and tears well up in my eyes. This truth speaks of security, it speaks of love, it speaks of favor, it speaks of rest, and it changes the focus from my activity to God's activity. Oh, how I need that focus—and I suspect others do, too.

I may never set a competitive foot on any kind of sports court. Because God has chosen me, I am left with only one thing to do: to enter *his* gates with thanksgiving and into *his* courts with praise because he has chosen me (Ps. 100:4; Col. 1:12).

## 45
## Free

August 1, 2014

Steve and I enjoyed a retreat to the city in July. For the last several years, we have made it our practice to get away alone together for a couple of days, and for some reason, we usually end up in a big city. We love our small town life, but we also love all the lights and activity of the city. These retreats provide ample time to relax without an agenda, to enjoy one another's company, and to talk extensively about our lives and priorities. Sometimes these getaways serve as a reset. Sometimes they just remind us to be more intentional in our relationship.

On our last retreat, as we strolled hand in hand into the *National Underground Railroad Freedom Center* in Cincinnati, OH I was not prepared to be shaken out of my idyllic retreat and into a time of sober contemplation. Thinking that we were going to learn more about the Underground Railroad and the struggle for freedom that black slaves went through, we instead walked directly into an exhibit on modern slavery.

I've lived a generally sheltered life full of first world problems, but I'm not completely naïve regarding the evil in the world. I've lived in Southern California and have seen the homeless, desperate people on the street. I've noticed from a young age the strip clubs and other places that exploit women. I've been in India and have seen firsthand the people who were missing limbs, thrown onto train tracks by their own parents to earn a better wage begging. I've been a pastor's wife and have listened to tales of lives destroyed by abuse, pornography, gambling, infidelity, and so much more. I've heard firsthand, and read, detailed stories of the intense persecutions of Christians. Yes, there is much evil in the world and it starts in the heart.

I know this. I've seen glimpses of it in my own life. I remember that, as a teenager, I killed my unborn baby for my own convenience and image. I recount the prideful, selfish, lazy moments that have littered my life and I know that there is a slavery that exists in modern day, an unseen slavery.

At the *Freedom Center* my eyes were opened a little wider to the reality of present day evil: sex trafficking, forced labor, and unfair and cruel treatment by one human being towards another human being. I was saddened almost to a point of weeping. The enormity of the problem was staring me in the face as I read statistics and stories, saw faces and imagined people created in God's image treating and being treated in the most horrible ways. I thought, "What am I to do about this?" I cannot stand idly by.

We moved on to another exhibit and saw the familiar story of the African slave trade. At one point in the exhibit the music overhead served to remind me of the answer to my earlier question. I heard the voices of African slaves soulfully humming *Amazing Grace*. Yes, of course! That reminded me of someone who was a wretch, lost and blind, but who was saved by the amazing grace of Jesus Christ. This man's life was transformed from slave trader to a pastor, and from selling people to writing one of the world's most well-known hymns. The story of John Newton, a man radically changed by God's merciful grace towards a sinner, reminds me that slavery is a horrible evil. Yet the deeper, and far vaster, slavery that often goes unseen is the slavery to sin. All people who have ever walked this planet have been enslaved to sin. All people who are currently walking this planet are born into slavery to sin. All people who will ever walk the dust of this earth will be enslaved to sin. Not just a portion of the population. Everyone.

O wretched humans that we are, who will rescue us from these bodies of death? Thanks be to God through Jesus Christ our Lord, he has bought our freedom (see Rom. 7:24–8:11).

I don't personally see much of the modern slave trade, but I pray for God to show me how to live my life in light of that reality.

The ultimate answer is to be continually reminded of the freedom that I have in Christ and to share that message of freedom with others. I agree with the quote I saw on the wall of the museum: "The function of freedom is to free someone else."[25] How am I living my life to see others freed from the bondage of sin? I am called to this location, this neighborhood, this family, and this church. This world is in bondage. How does the everyday life of a middle-aged woman participate in God's freedom crusade? That, my friends, is a matter for much prayer, much seeking the Lord, and a reminder to live more intentionally. I pray God will help me keep an eye to the cross and an eye to the spiritually enslaved all around me. I cannot muster up enough passion to keep me caring, but God certainly can, and I want him to sustain this passion in me. I want to care about freedom, not because I am a good person with a moral conscience, but because I have the Spirit of the living, freedom-loving God in me. He cares about freedom so much so that he went to great lengths to secure it for me. The perfect sinless Jesus Christ bought my freedom with the price of his own suffering, shame, rejection, cruel mistreatment, and punishment for sins he did not commit. He freed those who believe in and trust in Christ from bondage to sin. We now have freedom to choose not to sin. He freed us from the consequences of sin. Damnation and eternal separation from a holy and just God will never happen to us. He freed us from being enslaved by the efforts of trying earn God's mercy. He freed us from a life of futility.

Since visiting that exhibit, the question that keeps coming to my mind is this: "What will I do with my freedom?" My tendency is to come up with an action plan to get radical and change everything so that I will become some remarkable witness to the grace of God. Sometimes we need a kick in the behind like that. But perhaps the kick in the behind has more to do with our *ordinary* sustained obedience than our radical displays of obedience that cannot be sustained long term.

Steve has been preaching lately through the commands in Colossians 3. Keep in mind that these commands were issued to a people living in a world full of injustice and cruelty. Slavery then was not hidden; it was an ordinary way of life. God's commands to his people living in this culture were to challenge them to treat each other in ways that were counter-cultural. The commands had to do with what seems like ho-hum ordinary obedience in the midst of a culture that needed so many big revolutionary changes. We need to understand that to submit to our husbands, love our wives, obey our parents, obey our masters, and treat those under our authority with kindness is revolutionary! It's using our newfound freedom not as a license to live however we desire, but as an opportunity to serve a different master. Our freedom from sin is freedom from a cruel, insatiable master. Now we are free to obey the only master who is just, good, righteous, all-powerful, wise, kind, and loving. Now, we have hope to offer those around us who are enslaved as we once were.

How will you use your freedom?

## 46
## Trusting the Unshakable Refuge

September 13, 2014

Turn on any news channel and watch for more than 10 minutes, and you will see reasons to fret about what is going on in the world. Scroll down your social media page and most likely you will read something that stirs up your heart to feel sad, afraid, indignant, self righteous, or angry. Read the comment section on just about any opinion article and you may feel despair over the human race. There are troubling things going on around us. There are evil men on killing sprees. There is corruption in just about every organization. It seems as if immoral and godless people are getting the upper hand in our culture. You don't have to look very far to find people who are pointing out every error and reason to distrust leaders in the Christian community.

Open your Bible and you will soon come across records of the same. Evil men on killing sprees, corruption in kingdoms, immoral and godless people who seemed to have the upper hand for a time, and Christians who are in constant need of rebuke and instruction because of the sins they commit.

We may have more instant information today, but things have been the same since the fall of man. "There is nothing new under the sun," as Solomon declares (Eccl. 1:9). Sin lurks in hearts; it deceives and enslaves. Read history and you see this sad reality. Knowing this reality, however, certainly does not mean that we are not affected by it. We can recognize that there is "nothing new under the sun," but that does not change the grief that we feel when hard things touch our lives. What that knowledge can do, if we let it, is to remind us of our smallness, our lack of control, and our need to rely on something bigger than ourselves. It can give us perspective that the "here and now" will soon be "then and gone."

David, the king of Israel, had that perspective. He experienced evil first hand, not only in those around him, but also within himself. The Psalms he wrote are full of honest, practical help for us when we meet with evil. Psalm 37, for instance, reminds us that though the wicked seem to prosper, their day of judgment will come. David tells us to put our hope in the only sure refuge, the lord; Yahweh, Creator of heaven and earth.

What should our response be to the evil around us? Not fretting, not anger, not judgment, not envy (Ps. 37:1, 7–8). We must ask ourselves, "What good can fretting do?" According to this Psalm, it "only tends to evil" (Ps. 37:8). Rather, our response is meant to be one of trusting in the Lord (Ps. 37:3, 5), delighting in him (Ps. 37:4), committing our way to him (Ps. 37:5), waiting for him (Ps. 37:7, 34), taking refuge in him (Ps. 37:40), knowing his ways (Ps. 37:31), and following them (Ps. 37:34). I feel in my heart a resounding, "Yes, this is how I want to respond!"

Perhaps, like me, you feel your inability to perfectly respond like this.

For much of my life, I read these Psalms without finding the comfort they bring me now. Psalm 37 is full of statements about how the Lord will reward the righteous, the blameless, and those who keep his way (Ps. 37:17, 18, 21, 29, 30, 31, 32, 33, 37, 39, 40). When I read this Psalm before, my heart was full of self-righteousness because I was not as bad as "those other people," though I was also keenly aware of my failures to do all the right things. Though I had acknowledged Jesus as my Savior from sin, I had not realized that he was my Savior from my self-atoning, self-exalting, self-efforts at righteousness (which were also sin). When I read the Bible and saw the word, "righteous," I could be afraid that I was not righteous, because I was looking at my performance and evaluating myself. An admonition to "fret not" could cause more fretting in my core, because I could not perfectly keep myself from fretting or stay in a state of trusting, delighting, submitting, or following.

But God, in his mercy, opened my eyes to see *his* grace. A.W. Pink reminds us:

> *The grace of God is proclaimed in the Gospel (Acts 20:24), which is to the self-righteous Jew a "stumbling block," and to the conceited and philosophizing Greek "foolishness." And why so? Because there is nothing whatever in it that is adapted to the gratifying of the pride of man. It announces that unless we are saved by grace, we cannot be saved at all. It declares that apart from Christ, the unspeakable Gift of God's grace, the state of every many is desperate, irremediable, hopeless. The Gospel addresses men as guilty, condemned, perishing criminals. It declares that the chastest moralist is in the same terrible plight as is the most voluptuous profligate; and the zealous professor, with all his religious performances, is no better off than the most profane infidel.*[26]

At the foot of the cross, we are all on equal terms. We are all under the judgment of a holy and just God. On my own merit, I would fare no better there than the man on a killing spree, or the immoral godless ones who turn the tide of the culture, or the gossips and slanderers who delight in tearing down reputations. My attempts to be righteous are an affront to the only one who is truly righteous. They are tainted with pride on every level. Thank God they have nothing to do with my salvation (Eph. 2:8–9, and so many more verses)! Trusting that Jesus lived the righteous life that I could never live, and knowing that through his atoning death on the cross he gave me credit for it in exchange for all my evil deeds and sin-tainted good works, is the only way to find refuge (Ps. 37:40). It's the way out of fretting, because no matter what evil is being manifested in the world, my soul is secure. It's trusting, delighting, committing, and following Jesus, who for refuge I have fled. It's knowing that my salvation in this life and the life to come is from the Lord. He is my stronghold in the time of trouble. The Lord helps me, and delivers me from the wicked, and saves me, because I take refuge in him (from Ps. 37:39–40).

We can't bury our heads in the sand. Eventually, the news of our world will reach our ears and tempt us to fret. Jesus himself told us that in this world we will have trouble, but to take heart because he has overcome the world (John 16:33).

Whether it is the sin in our own hearts or the sin in the world that causes us to fret, the answer is the same: to look up and put our hope in God, the only One who does all things right and who will not act against his nature. We can trust that he will act and that his actions will be consistent with his holiness, his mercy, his patience, his love, his knowledge, his power, and all that he is. I cannot think of anything more comforting in a world that seems out of control! Let's not misplace our trust in the things that we see, but rather rightly place our trust in what God has said and declared himself to be in his infallible word.

## 47
## Always Learning

November 8, 2014

A few years ago, I met a woman who has led me by example in many ways. She showed me what it looks like to listen with grace and understanding, to give timely wisdom, to make others feel genuinely loved and cared for, to honor and respect my husband and to "love more than need" in my relationships. Perhaps the biggest thing I learned from her was to always be learning. Though she had more life experience than me she often made me feel as if she was learning from me and learning *with* me. Though she did not shy away from speaking God's truth to me, she would also embrace the mysteries that exist in life and tell me that we were "limping along together." Perhaps you have put a definition to this in your mind already. This example was one of humility.

I am not naturally humble. I'm sure my friend would tell you that she is not either. No one is naturally humble. By God's grace, little by little, teaching us the ways of humility is what God does in us as he transforms us into the image of his Son.

Anyone who has had teenagers and has tried to give them counsel has probably heard the phrase, "I know," at one time or another. I don't think I've outgrown that teenage tendency. I suspect that my kids probably picked up that phrase from me. It's a bad habit. I may not say it out loud all the time, but inside I often have an attitude of "I know." This means I resist receiving from others things that I may or may not have learned in the past. We all know many things, and we've experienced much, but we also are prone to forget. We are prone to take our eyes off of our Savior and the truth of God's word and put them onto a myriad of other things. We all need constant reminders of truth. This is a wonderful thing. It is a means of grace from God.

My friend taught me that learning, and relearning, is lifelong. I can listen to what others have to say, watch other's examples, and be spurred on by them. This is right and very good. I can choose to see all the grace in a person's life and celebrate that. Rather than see others as competition, I can see the beauty of the body of Christ in all of its diversity and share in (and benefit from) the ways

God has worked in others.

Our North American culture tends to be one of isolation, and greatly values independence and self-reliance, but these are not biblical values. God has called us into community, and more specifically into his church. The New Testament frequently speaks of the importance of the church and, in particular, the local expression of the body of Christ in which we are part of.

There is risk involved. I'd venture to say that most, if not all, of us have been hurt at one time or another by someone in church. Being real feels dangerous. Interestingly enough, there is much in the New Testament about forgiving; about loving those who have wronged you, about bearing with one another and being patient with one another. Can we acknowledge that as God allows us to be hurt by others, he also gives us the opportunity to put into practice all of those commands? If we did not need to deal with sinful people, we would not need to grow in those areas. It's precisely *because* we are sinful ourselves that we need to grow in these areas. We must trust that God's hand is at work among us, even when life is awkward or messy. Do we believe that we have much to learn from the everyday ordinary people that we rub shoulders with on a weekly basis in our church? Do we believe that God has sovereignly placed us in this particular church body to help fulfill his work in the life of another person and to have them help fulfill his work in us?

I don't want to shrink back because I've been burned before, and I don't want to assume that I know all I need to know in my own experiences. I want to grow in reaching out in vulnerability and trusting God for the outcome. I also want to grow in a life of humility that sees, celebrates, and learns from all that the grace of God is doing in my brothers and sisters in Christ.

I'd be grateful for more partners to run, walk, and limp along with me on this road to heaven. Will you join me? Let's always be learning!

# Appendix

The phrase *do the next thing* comes from the following poem. It often comes to mind when I feel overwhelmed.

Do The Next Thing

*From an old English parsonage, down by the sea,*
*There came in the twilight, a message to me;*
*Its quaint Saxon legend,*
*Deeply engraven,*
*Hath, as it seems to me,*
*Teaching from Heaven.*
*And on through the hours*
*The quiet words ring*
*Like a low inspiration-*
*DO THE NEXT THING*

*Many a questioning, many a fear,*
*Many a doubt, hath its quieting here.*
*Moment by moment,*
*Let down from Heaven,*
*Time, opportunity,*
*Guidance, are given.*
*Fear not tomorrows,*
*Child of the King,*
*Trust them with Jesus,*
*DO THE NEXT THING*

*Do it immediately;*
*Do it with prayer;*
*Do it reliantly, casting all care;*
*Do it with reverence,*
*Tracing His Hand,*
*Who placed it before thee with earnest command.*
*Stayed on Omnipotence,*
*Safe 'neath His wing,*

*Leave all resultings,*
*DO THE NEXT THING*

*Looking to Jesus, ever serener,*
*Working or suffering be thy demeanor,*
*In His dear presence,*
*The rest of His calm,*
*The light of His countenance*
*Be thy psalm,*
*Strong in His faithfulness,*
*Praise and sing,*
*Then, as He beckons thee,*
*DO THE NEXT THING*

*-Author unknown*

## Notes

1. Frances R. Havergal, "Like a River Glorious." Cyber Hymnal. http://cyberhymnal.org/htm/l/i/likriver.htm (retrieved November 14, 2014).
2. Scott Roley, *Things We Leave Behind*, Michael Card. © 1994 by Sparrow Music, MP4.
3. Thomas Wilcox, *Honey Out of the Rock*. (Pensacola: Chapel Library, Circa 1665), 11-12.
4. You can download or listen online to this sermon by Jeff Purswell at: http://sgclouisville.org/sovereign-grace-church-louisville-sermons/sermon/2013-03-24/counsel-for-the-christian-soul---philippians-4:4-7---jeff-purswell
5. A seminar attended that was based on the book by: Timothy S. Lane, and Paul David Tripp, *How People Change* (Greensboro: New Growth Press 2008).
6. *North and South*, DVD, directed by Brian Percival (2004; Burbank, CA: BBC Warner Video, 2005).
7. Bill Moore and Henry Lyte, *Jesus I My Cross Have Taken*, Various Artists. © 2010 by Indelible Grace Music, MP4.
8. Dorothy Frances Gurney. *"God's Garden."* Poet's Corner. http://www.theotherpages.org/poems/gurney01.html (retrieved November 14, 2014).
9. Tim Hughes and Martin Smith. *Clinging to the Cross*. Tim Hughes and Brooke Fraser. © 2007 by Thankyou Music. MP4.
10. Matthew Henry, *"Isaiah 7,"* Bible Study Tools. http://www.biblestudytools.com/commentaries/matthew-henry-complete/isaiah/7.html (retrieved November 17, 2014).
11. Ibid
12. Andreé Seu, "Seventeen Minutes," in *World Magazine,* June 2005, http://www.worldmag.com/2005/06/seventeen_minutes.
13. Sam Storms, *The Hope of Glory* (Wheaton: Crossway Books, 2007), 231.
14. Ibid, 253.

15 Joni Eareckson Tada, *Pearls of Great Price: 366 Daily Devotional Readings* (Grand Rapids: Zondervan Publishing, 2006), NP (January 16).

16 Arthur Bennett, ed., *The Valley of Vision* (Edinburgh: Banner of Truth Trust), p. (Page 5). © 1975, used by permission. www.banneroftruth.org

17 Ibid, 5.

18 Samuel Rodigast, 1676, Translated by Catherine Winkworth, 1863. Music and alternate words by Mark Altrogge, *Whatever My God Ordains is Right*, Stephen Altrogge (In a Little While, © 2007 Sovereign Grace Praise).

19 George Mueller, *A Narrative of Some of the Lords Dearlings* (London: J. Nisbet & Co., 1860) 405.

20 Bennett, *The Valley of Vision*, 55.

21 Jerry Bridges, *Respectable Sins* (Colorado Springs: NavPress, 2007), 54.

22 You can read about the ministry of Dr. John Piper at www.desiringgod.org. His ministry is founded on the statement: "God is most glorified in us when we are most satisfied in him."

23 Eareckson Tada, *Pearl of Greatest Price*, May 10.

24 Content. Dictionary.com. The American Heritage® Dictionary of Idioms by Christine Ammer. Houghton Mifflin Company. http://dictionary.reference.com/browse/content (accessed: November 17, 2014).

25 This was a quote by author Toni Morrison displayed at the "National Underground Railroad Freedom Center," in Cincinnati, OH. Visit freedomcenter.org for more information.

26 Arthur W. Pink, *The Attributes of God,* (Grand Rapids: Baker Books, 2006), 70.

Made in the USA
San Bernardino, CA
09 December 2016